ANIMAL WISDOM
Communications With Animals

5/1/09

To Tricia

Enjoy their

wisdom

Anita

D0910520

ANIMAL WISDOM
Communications With Animals

Anita Curtis

iUniverse.com, Inc.
San Jose New York Lincoln Shanghai

Animal Wisdom
How to Hear the Animals

Published by iUniverse.com, Inc.

For information address:
iUniverse.com, Inc.
5220 S 16th, Ste. 200
Lincoln, NE 68512
www.iuniverse.com

Originally published by Self

ISBN: 0-595-18022-1

Printed in the United States of America

But ask now the beasts, and they shall teach you;
and the fowls of the air, and they shall tell you;
Or speak to the earth, and it shall teach you;
and the fishes of the sea shall declare to you.

Job 12:7-8

It is through a mystical communication
with animals
that the power of the human spirit is
preserved.

Unknown

Foreword

Anita's work has added so much to so many lives. She has given credence to our intuitions, made us listen and think. She has been an invaluable help and comfort to me and many in my practice. She has saved [animals] lives, time and [owners] expense.

Her matter-of-fact style of dealing with her work and the subjects of this writing (which are all to often rendered unbelievable by popular jargon) is a joy.

Anita has given us, and our animals, proof of a connection so important and so real and thereby has relieved the pain of "not being heard."

Judith Shoemaker, D.V.M.
Veterinarian
Doug Hannum's Sports Therapy and Training Center
Nottingham, Pennsylvania

TABLE OF CONTENTS

PART I

Collections

PART II

Individuals

Introduction

A book is seldom written straight through from beginning to end. You do a little here...and then a little there. One morning I looked at all the *book papers* spread around and had a feeling of overwhelming depression. I wondered who I thought I was, daring to write a BOOK! What right did I have?...and so on. Then Porcia, a horse, you will meet in Part II, made herself known. I share her words with you:

"If the book is no good no one will buy it. But, you have excellent help in all areas - and you are good." Porcia quietly chided. "People have to know we can think and feel. This is a vehicle of knowledge. Have we not given you organizational instructions, oh foolish doubting one? You must work hard and carry this message."

I quietly thanked Porcia and now continue my work of getting this book to you - the potential readers and existing or future animal communicators.

Once we had a dog that did not like rainy weather. The next dog to join our family loved the rain, and delighted in splashing in puddles.

Two of our chickens were setting on eggs that hatched the same day. One of the chickens took one look at the chicks and walked away. The other hen gathered *all* the chicks to her and cared for them.

We had a cat that loved to be outdoors. He would come in the house to gulp down some food, and ask to be let out again as soon as he had cleaned the crumbs from his whiskers. His successor wanted to stay in the house, no matter how balmy the day was.

Animal wisdom, animal personalities, animal traits are as varied as those of their human counterparts. There are countless instances where animals show their likes and dislikes, have their good days and bad, reveal their innate talents and their strengths and weaknesses - therefore it stands to reason they must be able to think and rationalize. They also have positive and negative feelings, including: joy, love, dislike, and even impassivity, as in the case of the not-so-maternal chicken.

Years of animal research show that animal parents (or in some instances only the female of the species) love and care for their young. Some birds act injured and put themselves in danger so that a predator will follow them away from the nest. Other animals mate for life, or form bonds that are so deep if one dies, the other will be deeply depressed - sometimes to the point of its own death from loneliness.

I never doubted that animals think and feel. I just didn't consciously realize that they could tell you their thoughts and feelings. When I found out that it was possible to communicate through such channels as words, feelings, and images, to name a few, I was anxious to explore the world of animal/human communications.

I never imagined that there would come a point where I would spend a good portion of each day doing animal communication consultations, by telephone, from my office with clients and their animals. I now have regular office hours, filled with appointments for animal communication consultations.

The thought that veterinarians could call me to ask a question that would *help* with their diagnoses (*I do not diagnose*), never entered my mind.

Animal communications has become my career. I not only have the pleasure of communicating daily with numerous animal friends and helping them with their communications with their people companions. I also frequent the lecture circuit discussing animal communications with wonderfully varied audiences from sophisticated veterinarians, to dedicated groups of pot bellied pig companions. I make guest appearances on television and radio and am quoted frequently in articles on animal communications for leading pet related publications. Best of all I lead workshops and seminars to teach other people how to communicate with their animal companions.

Of all the groups I work with, the group I have the most outstanding respect for are the veterinarians. It is difficult enough to work in the medical field, let alone to practice with patients who can't readily tell you what hurts and where. My awe and admiration is clearly evident with all members of the medical field. This book is in no way intended to suggest that animal communications can take the place of veterinary care, instead it strongly suggests that the animal wisdom through communications can possibly help situations.

An animal communicator is often called when the veterinarian has tried all of the routine and/or intuitive ways of treating the animal and there is still need for improvement. At this time the animal can give the communicator additional information such as: where the pain is, what it feels like, or possibly where it originates.

Some places in this book will indicate that the veterinarian had not been able to help the animal. I am not trying to imply that there was not adequate and responsible care, just that there was something else that did not show up.

A while back, I was invited to be a guest at an animal clinic at Doug Hannum's Sports Therapy and Training Center which is located near our Pennsylvania home, to watch Judith Shoemaker, D.V.M. She was gracious enough to invite me to be there to validate the information I receive from the animals. With the success of the first visit, Dr. Shoemaker has invited me to return on numerous occasions. Those days are unbelievably rewarding to me as I get immediate feedback from the animal and the veterinarian.

Please continue to always give your animal companion proper veterinary care, good nutrition, and exercise!

I have learned much from veterinarians who have been kind enough to share from their experience. I was on a radio program in Delaware with Dr. Jim Berg. People were calling in with questions about their animals.

One woman called with a common problem, her cat had suddenly stopped urinating in the litter box. I asked if the cat had been declawed, as it is not unusual for a declawed cat to not like coarse litter.

The cat had been declawed, but the litter was the very fine sand type. The cat had decided to join in on the call when she realized she was the reason for this desperate call. As the cat was telling me that it did not like the "smell," the woman was telling me that she kept the box "immaculate." I had no reason to believe that either one was not giving accurate information.

At that point Dr. Berg had some suggestions. Since the cat urinated in many different places on the rug, he suggested putting small bowls of food at those places. Cats will seldom urinate or defecate where they eat. He also suggested that the caller place several litter pans around the house, and make sure they were not too high for the cat to jump into them.

Dr. Berg also asked if the litter the woman was using was perfumed...cats often don't like the smell. *Lightbulb*! That was the answer that the cat had been telling me, now I understood what it was communicating, through the cat's frame of reference.

I suddenly realized that as my information comes from the animals they do not always have the solution, or we humans may not always understand their communication methods. Sometimes when a cat complains, he just wants it fixed! His idea of fixing a litter box problem can be to not use it anymore, then, by his standards, the problem is solved.

When I took my first tenuous steps along the path of animal communications I thought I might find out how my horse was feeling, or why my dog was barking, or even better, to ask her to stop barking. Little did I know that I was going to meet animals who were wise and spiritual, or who were so in tune with their bodies that they could even give descriptions of what was going on in their blood stream. I have also encountered animals who could tell what was going on in the bodies of other animals who lived far away from them.

There is no limit to what the mind can do. Open your own mind and hear the words of the animals!

My History

When I was a child, if anyone had asked me what I wanted to be when I grew up I would not have said, "An animal communicator." Many years later I can't imagine doing anything else. I have always loved animals, I began riding at an early age and felt a true bond with not only the rented horse I always rode and thought of as 'mine,' but all the animals in the stable. However, I would be destined to wait until I was fifty-five years old to find out that one could consciously communicate with animals.

Today I live with my family on a lovely patch of ground in eastern Pennsylvania. We have always shared our acreage with many animal companions. When I began exploring animal communications, we were living with a delightful horse, Colonel and a dear old pony, Sally. Although Sally is no longer with us, having died several years ago, our home is now graced with two additional horses, and several cats, Seven and Huit (eight in French).

As I sat one day reading the newspaper, an article caught my eye about a woman and her dog, who had been guests on a leading television program. As the story described the event, she had pieces of paper pinned to a clothes line. The papers had large numbers on them. She asked the dog to get her the paper that had the total of three and five. The dog brought her the paper with an eight on it. She then described a man in the audience and told the dog to take the paper to him, which the dog did.

The talk show host asked how she trained the dog. She explained it wasn't any particular training, but rather that she *thought* in pictures. The dog *read* those pictures and did what she asked. I was fascinated.

Later that morning, I went to the barn to clean the stalls of our horse, Colonel, and pony, Sally. The barn was built in the pasture so the animals could come in or stay out according to their own wishes. When they saw me walking to the barn they immediately started to walk to the stalls in hopes of convincing me to feed them a second breakfast or at the very least to bring some carrot treats.

I had not brought carrots and had no intention of providing them with a second breakfast, but neither did I want them in the barn making my chore more complicated.

I thought of the article I had just completed, and decided I had nothing to lose by trying to send them a message to stay out of my way. I had no idea how the woman had done it, so I just closed my eyes, took a deep breath, and got a mental image of both animals standing outside of the door, giving me enough room to walk in with the wheelbarrow.

When I came around the side of the barn, pushing the wheelbarrow, there they stood. Right where I had seen them in my mind! I was thrilled, but not for long. I decided it must be a coincidence. As I filled the wheelbarrow I could look out of the door and see Colonel standing across the doorway. I could see his body, but not his head or tail. Once again I closed my eyes, took a deep breath, and pictured him walking in a circle to look in the door. About ten seconds went by and then he walked in a circle and looked in the door.

This time my elation lasted a few seconds longer. But, I again decided it was a coincidence. He just wanted to know how soon he could beg for oats. No, it couldn't be. I looked out again, and he had returned to his headless, tailless position across the doorway.

He had just looked in...would he do it again...I had to know.

Okay, close eyes, breathe deeply, picture the action, wait...he did it!

I vacillated between believing and not believing. I would pitch a few forkfuls of straw into the wheelbarrow and then tell myself it was all coincidence. I kept asking him to do more things. "Just one more thing. Please take three steps, starting with your right front foot."

Right foot, three steps. Yes, we were communicating!

And then again I'd vision "Just one more thing. Please take three steps, starting with your left front foot."

Left front foot, three steps. Yes, this really was happening! I couldn't get enough.

I did a little more work and then filled with doubt, mucking stalls can do that to a person. "Just one more thing. Please turn your head and look at me."

I one-more-thinged the poor horse for about half an hour, but Colonel has always been kind and patient. I was finally finished with my cleaning chore and was sitting on the step at the stall entrance. Colonel and I were close enough to almost be touching; the pony, who had been observing all of the action, was now standing behind him with her knees locked while she dozed.

"Just one more thing," I asked, "If this is real, please touch my cheek with your nose."

Although I had done all of the closed eyes, deep breath routine, it just wasn't working. The sweet old horse just stared at me.

The third time I tried, Sally, the pony, bobbed her head as she woke from her nap, she walked around Colonel to where I sat, touched her nose to my cheek, and rolled her eyes at him. She then resumed her previous position and returned to her nap. I could only imagine that my mental pictures were disturbing her sleep!

Was it coincidence when a few days later a friend of mine called and said that a person was coming from California to Virginia to teach a workshop on how to do animal communications? She thought it sounded interesting and asked if I was interested in joining her. You can imagine my astonishment and excitement.

Jeri Ryan, Ph.D., was the workshop instructor. She is an associate of Penelope Smith, who I soon discovered is the leading pioneer in animal communications. We immediately registered for the class and were told to read Penelope's book *Animal Talk: Interspecies Communication* prior to arriving for the workshop as it would be used as a reference.

The day of the workshop, there were about eight people in the room, along with some dogs, cats, and birds. An African Grey parrot who had pulled his tail feathers out was in a cage, but a gorgeous blue macaw walked around the room asking each of us, "Do you want some supper?" When he got to me, he said, "Do you want some?"

"Some what?" I mentally asked him.

"Supper," came the quick reply. I wondered if it would all be that easy.

My fears were laid to rest. Nothing was difficult. The morning was pleasant as we introduced ourselves and told the others what we hoped to accomplish. We were then led through a meditation that allowed us to become an animal and understand what it was like to live in that body.

For our first exercise, Jeri told us to choose an animal, but if one came into mind, go with that one. I am only five-foot-four, and according to my weight, could really be much taller, so I thought it would be nice to be in the body of a gazelle. Maybe a deer would come to me so I would know what it would be like to leap and run. Perhaps a darling little dik dik that I've seen on *National Geographic*, leaping and bouncing through the forest would allow me to see the world through its eyes, and feel the lightness of its tiny body.

No such luck, I closed my eyes and came face-to-face with an elephant!

I was disappointed at first, but as I slipped into it's dense body, I soon felt quite at home. As Jeri led the meditation I was able to view life in that huge, gentle form. I could even see myself in a shallow pool, and feel the coolness of the water coming from my trunk and over my body. It was refreshing and fun.

We shared our experiences and then went on with the next exercise, which was learning to listen. Working in pairs, we were asked to recall times when we had admired an animal, or one had admired us. Times when we understood an animal, or one had understood us. There were quite a few sets of questions, and we were either telling of a time, or listening to our partner speak. We were not to judge, comment, or talk. Just listen. This was not easy for some of us, and I was not fully aware of why we were doing it. When I later did communicate with the animals I realized the value of *learning to just listen.*

The next segment was fun. Once again we sat in pairs, facing each other. Jeri led us through a meditation and prepared us to send images to each other. We had our eyes closed, so we could not see body language or facial expressions, yet we were all able to send and receive images. I was amazed at the accuracy in that little group of strangers. I knew from my experiment with our horse and pony that I was able to send messages, but now I started to believe that I could also receive them.

A lunch break was next on the agenda, and I could hardly wait for it to finish so we could move along to the next segment of the workshop.

As we gathered for the afternoon session which included actually speaking to the animals, Jeri refreshed our memories about the meditations, and how to open ourselves to accept the information. We were to be respectful, say "please" and "thank you."

I chose a stoic cat who had been watching the proceedings all morning. As instructed, I asked simple questions. "May I speak to you?" The cat blinked, so I took that for a positive answer. After all, he didn't get up and walk away. "How are you?"

"Quite well, thank you." He had answered! No, I made it up. I actually heard the cat's response in my mind. I looked at the other people in the room, expecting them to respond to my communication, but they were all staring at some winged or furred creature.

When we gathered to share our experiences, I decided to wait until some of the others had talked as I knew they would be green with envy. I got over that idea quickly as the other participants began to share their conversations. Several told of illnesses that the animals had at some time, which the attending owners confirmed. Others told of the animals personal likes and dislikes, and again the owners of those animals confirmed. When it was my turn I just said I had done quite well. I really felt like I had been in a pre-kindergarten section of the workshop.

I was licking my mental wounds when someone asked Jeri the question that shocked me. Did Jeri think the parrot's problem came from a past-life connection with the person who now had the bird? *Past life? Nobody asked questions like that! I considered myself very open-minded, but I certainly would not blurt something like that out in a room full of strangers. Probably not in a room full of friends, either. What was she thinking?*

Jeri calmly responded, "Yes." She went on to give the time period of the particular life involved. Everyone seemed comfortable with Jeri's remarks, with the exception of the open-minded one, **me**. *What was I doing here? Did I believe all of this?*

I had a lot to think about on my trip home from Virginia to Pennsylvania, and think I did. By the time I got home I couldn't wait to practice on any animal who would give me permission to talk to him. If past lives came up, so be it.

Some Very Personal Animal Friends

My mother would often tell the story of the Great Dane who lived in our neighborhood when I was a toddler in a quiet Philadelphia row house neighborhood. As the story went, one day we were sitting in front of our neighbor's house, as was the custom. The Great Dane wandered up the street and joined the ladies. I went to him, threw my arms around his neck, and said, "Nice horsie." When the Dane stood up and walked away I was still dangling from his neck saying, "Nice horsie."

My mother plucked me off of the dog, but I never got over wanting to be near horses.

Since my mother was terrified of horses, being near this object of my affection seemed remote. However, being a determined youngster, I knew that I wanted to be around horses, and I wasn't going to let anyone's fear stand in my way. I begged and pleaded to go riding whenever the opportunity arose. I was seven years old when my mother finally relented.

Exasperated with my determination, my mother suggested that my father could take me to the local stable to rent a horse. She knew once I got on one I would be so scared that I would never ask again. *Wrong!*

In those days it cost $1.25 an hour to rent a horse. That was a lot of money for us at the time. Saturday morning, as early as I could get my father there, we showed up at the stable. Although I would have been there at five in the morning on the appointed day, my father made me wait until they opened at nine.

I breathed in deeply and loved the smell of the place. The little pinto, Suzie, was led out for me. Once astride that small mare I felt on top of the world, and I never wanted to step back down. After the ride I was still excited. My father and I went home and in my excitement I was able to convince my mother to go back with us to see the horses.

She went reluctantly, but refused to leave the car. She even locked the doors in case one of the horses wanted to try to get in. By this time I was an expert in my own mind, and I was telling her everything there was to know about horses and riding. In actuality, I had not gone faster than a walk, but that did not matter to me.

The following Saturday we dragged my mother along so she could watch us mount, leave the stable yard, and then an hour later, ride back in and dismount. The stable owner saw three people, and led out three horses. My mother was too shocked to be able to protest, and the next thing she knew she was sitting on a horse as he ambled along in line behind the guide and my father's horse. I brought up the rear with Suzie.

My mother was so stiff and sore that she could barely move all week. But, Saturday morning we dragged her back to the barn to ride. My mother spent about eight weeks in pain until she let go of some of her fear and learned to relax.

Years later she would own a horse. In fact, her horse, Smoky, was the first animal that I could communicate with, although I didn't realize it at the time.

I stopped after work at the hairdresser's shop one Friday for my regular appointment. As I walked through the door I had this nagging sense I needed to go home. At that time, if you had a *regular* appointment at the hairdresser, nothing stood in the way of your being there, so I tried to put the sense out of my mind. After all I didn't want to loose my coveted time slot.

As I patiently waited my turn, I couldn't put this sense out of my mind. In fact it became more and more overpowering. Finally I left the shop. Friday or not, I couldn't sit still.

When I arrived home I raced directly to the barn and found Smoky in the feed room. He was blind in one eye and couldn't see to turn around, so he was frightened and stuck. He had not been able to get into the feed bin, but he was scared - at that point I realized it was Smoky who had sent for me.

There were many times that Smoky let me know that there was a problem. Although my theory then was that we were on the same wave length, I thought that only he could communicate with me. Now I realize that those communications are a two-way street.

When my husband, Vic, and I bought a house with ground and a small barn, Smoky came to live with us and always brought us joy. Since he lived to be over thirty years old, we were able to enjoy many happy years together.

The dog companion who lived with us when I actually *learned* to communicate was a lovely Irish Setter/Black Labrador mix. As a puppy she was very awkward and prone to tripping, falling, or walking into things. While trying to decide what to name her, my son and I watched her miss a step and fall off our back steps. My son said, "Here comes Clumsy."

We thought that was so funny that we named her Clumsy. I cannot tell you how much I regret that. When I could talk to her I learned, in no uncertain terms, that she did not like that name. She told me that "Clums" was acceptable, but that her true name was Persian Princess. That was a long name, and we were not expected to call her that, but she wanted us to know that *Persian Princess was her given name.*

My husband shared her dislike of Clumsy, and called her Puppy. I have chosen to refer to her as Puppy in this book and hope it will help to atone for my ignorance. I apologized to her, and she assured me that she understood and forgave me. She was sweet and fun loving, not one to carry a grudge.

One night, when she was twelve years old, Puppy looked at me and told me that her heart and lungs were causing her so much distress that she did not want to go on living. I had been dreading this day, but I had promised to help her if she asked. We called the veterinarian and lifted her into the back of the car. I sat with her and held her, explaining what I knew of what she was about to experience. She was calm and unafraid, and it was the only time in her life that she did not shake uncontrollably in the veterinarian's office.

We miss her so, even years after her passing, but when Vic and I walk on a certain part of our property we know she is with us. She used to dash off to chase critters, return to check in, and be off again. At times we both look to the same spot at the same time, and we know she is *checking in.*

At one time we had about twenty chickens. Every now and then one of the hens would decide she wanted a family. We did not have a rooster, but once when this happened I went to the hatchery and bought some fertile eggs to put under the hen, and a few days later they hatched. The proud mother believed they were her own offspring and raised them well. One of the chicks was a male who turned into a beautiful rust brown rooster with bright white feathers around his neck like a collar. He became the protector of the flock, and when a stranger came near the chicken run, or near the hens when they were out of the run, he herded them into a corner and became ready to defend them.

I watched the rooster several times as he found a group of insects or seeds. He would cluck in a certain way to the 'ladies' and they would run to where he was to enjoy the feast he had discovered and provided for them. Even though I did not know about animal communication at the time we had the chickens, it seemed quite natural to me that he could do that. After all, they all spoke the same language. However, when the rooster and Puppy interacted I was more surprised.

The rooster and Puppy used to have confrontations that went on and on. Puppy would have her nose about six inches from the rooster's beak, and she would bark in a slow cadence. The loud "Woo, Woo, Woo" would continue until the rooster got fed up. He would then stretch his neck, spread his wings, and chase her.

Puppy would run, while looking back over her shoulder, until the rooster stopped. Then she would turn and we would hear the "Woo, Woo, Woo" again. Vic and I used to feel sorry for the rooster and call her away, but a few minutes later the sound of her barking would fill the air again.

One day Puppy and I were walking by the chicken run and I heard a short "Cluck." Puppy turned toward the fence and was face to face with the rooster. He made the sound again and Puppy started her barking. Then I understood that there was a communication going on between them. The rooster was obviously calling her a name, and she was reacting. I realized that we had been feeling sorry for the rooster in error. He had riled her each time, and it was their game. I never interfered with them again.

When I began to have some unexplained abdominal pains ten years ago I began to wonder what the possible cause of the pains could be. I did not have a horse at the time, only Sally, our pony, who did not wander far from the barn much anymore.

As I looked out the window at the empty pasture I had a yearning to have a horse once more. Being a fatalist, as I nursed my abdominal pains, thinking the worst, I knew I did not want to end my days looking at that horseless field.

I looked at some livestock ads in the paper and saw one for a horse. It was the day after Thanksgiving so I had the day off.

I went to see the horse, and immediately fell in love with Colonel. The seller told me that he could not be tied, but was a perfect horse otherwise. He was used to carrying even the most timid rider. He was in a medium-sized box stall, and had a paddock that was nothing but mud. Although he was clean and well fed, the sparkle in his eye, that said he was happy, was missing.

Since my plan was to ride often, I thought Colonel and I needed to see how we felt about each other. It was opening day of hunting season as we meandered up the street. I could hear the shots being fired in the fields nearby. Colonel did not blink, wiggle his ears, or react in any way. I bought him! Years later, Colonel and I were chatting and he said in a matter-of-fact tone, "By the way, do you realize I'm deaf?" To my amazement, I wasn't aware of this fact, since Colonel and I communicated telepathically it never made any difference to our communications.

When Colonel was delivered to our home we led him into the grassy pasture. He dropped his head and began eating the grass as fast as he could. He did not even notice Sally as she came rushing around the side of the barn to see who dared to come on to her property. She snorted and stamped her little hoof, and Colonel was oblivious to her as he ate the grass. When he finally raised his head to look at Sally she saw that he was no threat to her, so she joined him in his feast. They were inseparable till the day she died.

Colonel is always very quiet. He never whinnies, just gives a low throaty nicker when he sees us. The day little Sally passed away we had to get a truck in to remove her remains. Colonel watched everything, and as the truck pulled away he trumpeted a loud whinny of good-by. He was very lonely for the first few weeks, but there were new friends on the horizon who would be joining him in the near future.

Colonel is over thirty years old now, and starting to show signs of his advanced age. I cherish every minute we have together and have never regretted buying him. The sparkle is always dancing in his dreamy eyes. At least I know he has had over ten years in a happy home.

As I remember the animals Vic and I have been fortunate enough to share our home with over the years, I realize that there was constant communications going on that I was not aware of at the time. After I learned how to channel my thoughts better, and receive the thoughts the animals were sending I began to realize the reality of all this communication.

Little Sally was the one, however, that sent the most unusual message. When she was quite old one of the horse feed companies developed a product that was for the geriatric group of horses. I bought a bag of the feed and gave Sally a sample. When I asked her if she liked it she said, "It makes water in my mouth."

I didn't know what she meant, and I started to worry that she would choke. All of a sudden I realized that when I think of my favorite food I can feel extra water in my mouth. Sally was telling me that she liked the feed, but in a special way. Since I had not understood her message at first, I knew it was not something I had made up, or something I would have wanted her to say.

Sally was always wise and wonderful.

Animal Communications...
What Is It?

If you watch fish swimming in a tank you can see that they all turn at once, as do flocks of birds as they fly. Herds of galloping deer, horses, cattle, make the same sudden turns as they run. I doubt if one cries out, "Quick, left turn. Pass it on...!" There is a mental communication instead.

When I first became seriously interested in developing my skills as an animal communicator to better tap into the wisdom of these wonderful companions, I was fortunate to be introduced to the studies of Penelope Smith, perhaps the foremost animal communicator and pioneer in the field. She has tapes on this subject, and her book *Animal Talk: Interspecies Communication* explains in depth the process of animal communications.

Since my book is not a how-to on communications, but rather to share the wisdom of some of the many animals with whom I have had the pleasure of communicating, I don't want to get into specifics, but I will touch on some of the process.

There are meditations and mental exercises to help you clear your mind, to enable you to become one-with-an-animal, and to help you listen. The exercises are all important, but fine tuning the listening is something many of us don't do. Our minds race ahead of the speaker, organizing what we are going to say as soon as he or she stops talking. (When I am communicating with an animal I feel what the animal feels by telepathically becoming one with him. When the animal gives permission for communication, I telepathically slip into the animal's body and we become as one.)

Another part of learning is an exercise that has you sending an image to another person while you are sitting opposite each other. Each person has closed eyes, and is listening to the workshop leader take them through the meditation, and guide them through the exercise.

When I am teaching a workshop, I love seeing the reactions of the participants when they compare what was sent, and how well the information was received. So many people come to a workshop with the attitude of "...maybe everyone else can do this, but I know I won't be able to." (*Actually, I had a bit of that skepticism when I attended my first workshop.*) Then they find that they can send and receive information telepathically, and the energy in the room becomes charged and the students become enthusiastic.

I am delighted at every workshop I give when I see the transformation of the group as they realize that they have sent messages to a person who cannot see facial expressions or body language - or they have received an image under those conditions.

I believe we all have the ability to learn how to communicate because we all used mental telepathy millions of years ago when our vocal cords were not evolved to the condition they are in now. There are tribes of Aborigines in Australia that still communicate telepathically.

Since most human communications have evolved through spoken words, mental telepathy is no longer developed. The wiring in our brain that enables us to transfer thoughts is still there, just laying dormant and covered with grey dust.

The exercises that Penelope Smith has developed allows one to dust off these wires, make sure the connections are secure, and use them again. Now we can communicate with the animals who have been using telepathy all of their lives.

Animals do not usually seem surprised when they are contacted telepathically. They are often delighted that they can finally be understood. After all, they have understood us for years.

Hindsight is said to be 20/20. I know now that over the years I carried on communications with many animals. Once I learned the techniques of animal communications, all those experiences made sense. Now I can't imagine life without talking with the animals.

As I have mentioned, I take great joy in teaching workshops. When leading the participants through a meditation and giving them a color to image, it is always a thrill to see them receive it. This is an activity where the group has split into partners and send the images to each other. Some groups enjoy this activity so much that they ask to do it a few more times.

This happened at one workshop where I had already told the group to use the color green. When we did the exercise the second time I used the color green again. Two young women were sitting facing each other. When I told them to compare what image was sent and what was received, I could hear the excitement in their voices. The sender was the same person who was the sender when we used the color green the first time. When I told them to form an image of an object that was the green color, the sender thought to herself, "I'll send a green leaf. Oh, wait, I sent a green leaf the last time. This time I'll send grass."

When they made the comparison the receiver told the sender - word for word - what she had thought about the leaf and the grass.

We were working on the same exercise at another workshop and I had told the group to send an image of an object that was brown. We had an odd number of participants at that workshop, and there was one group with three people in it. Ouida George was the sender, and when I said to use brown she thought of a pair of brown shoes, but dismissed the idea in favor of boots. She thought, "I'll throw one boot to Maire, and one to Carolyn," and then she formed an image of one boot being tossed to each of them.

When they compared, Carolyn was laughing and said she could see a brown boot flying at her. Maire said that she saw a brown shoe, and then the images started changing and she could not tell what it turned into.

I asked who had the left, and who had the right. Carolyn had the left boot, and Maire had the right shoe. That was the way Ouida had sent them!

Part of my enjoyment of facilitating workshops is because they are made up of a group of people who are anxious to learn how to communicate with their animal companions, and the energy is high and positive. One time, however, the excitement came from one of the dogs.

Ronni Yaskin had lost her beloved dog Belker a little over a month before the workshop. The workshop was Ronni's second one, so she was already able to communicate with Belker, but wanted to hone her skills.

When Ronni sat down, Riley, a setter/lab mix who had come as a working model for our workshop, stared at the space beside Ronni's leg, and wagged his tail. Then his tail suddenly stopped...he sniffed the air and looked rather confused. He repeated this several times, then he turned and climbed onto his person's lap, put his front paws on her shoulders, and tried to climb the wall to look in the mirror. He stretched as far as he could and stared into the mirror, looking toward Ronni's reflection.

He knew there was a dog with Ronni, but could not get it's scent. He spent a good portion of the day trying to figure out how to get to know the "phantom dog" better. We told him it was Belker, but he kept trying to get the more physical connections.

Belker had other things on his mind, and ignored Riley. He had told Ronni that he would be at the workshop with her and would prove it. He said she would get the same message three times. We did not know what that meant at first, but Ronni recognized when it happened. Belker had earlier discussed the possibility of returning to Ronni as a bird, and three different times, one right after another, someone in the room sent Ronni an image of a bird. Ronni was then confident that Belker was behind the three birds, and was indeed with her. Of course Riley's actions gave even more credence to the experience.

Dowsing

One of the tools that I have discovered to be useful to me in my work with animal communications is dowsing. I have found it to be particularly helpful when trying to locate missing animals. I also feel that when you begin to open your mind to skills that are unusual, it is beneficial to explore other abilities that are also laying dormant deep within.

There is no end to the adventurous road we travel, and dowsing is something that we can learn and practice easily. There are many good books on how to dowse, but I will give a brief explanation. Some people feel that we all have the knowledge of the Universe within us and dowsing is the key to unlock that knowledge.

For my personal dowsing work, I have an old lead fishing sinker hanging by a thin black string. It is kept on a hook on my computer hutch. I keep it handy so it is always available when I need it.

I carry a teardrop crystal pendant in my pocketbook. I use it because it is pretty and flashes colors as it swings, not because it gives me clearer information. If I am not near my lead sinker or crystal, I use whatever is handy: car keys on a rubber band, jewelry, or anything else that has some weight to it and can swing. It does not seem to matter what the weighted object is made of, or if it is balanced.

My *high tech* dowsing rods are made up of a wire coat hanger that has been cut in three places. I used to use small tree branches, but I stopped because there are enough other materials around, so I prefer not to inflict pain on the tree.

To make a simple pendant for yourself:
1) Tie a string to an object.
2) Hold the string between your thumb and index finger, support the string with the fingers of your other hand, and allow the string to lower slowly. At some point the pendant may start to turn or swing. That is the length that is best for you, so tie a knot in the string, and that is where you hold it when you ask questions.

If you try a couple of times, and the pendant does not turn, just hold the string in a place that seems more comfortable for you.

You are now ready to begin the dowsing:

- First, I prop my elbow on something so that my arm does not get tired, hold the string in my fingers, close my eyes, and take three deep breaths. I then picture myself in a place that brings me serenity, or with people that I love, or both.

- Then I open my eyes and ask the pendant, "Please show me a *Yes*." The pendant should start to swing, either vertically, horizontally, on an angle, or in a circle. It may be a small movement at first, but you should be able to see the direction.
- Ask the pendant, "Please stop."
- When it does, ask, "Show me a *No*." The pendant should go off in a different direction.

When you ask a question, your answers are shown to you by the *Yes* or *No* direction of the pendant. Now ask some questions that you know the answers to, such as, "Is my name Anita Curtis?"

I expect to get a *Yes* response to that question, but you expect to get a *No* - unless there is another Anita Curtis out there. If there is, drop me a line to say "Hi."

Be sure to ask one question at a time. To ask, "Will I take a test tomorrow and will I pass it?" break this down into two separate questions. "Will I take a test tomorrow?" and then "Will I pass it?"

You can also ask about numbers by asking, for instance, "Is the amount between ten and twenty?" "Is the amount between twenty-one and thirty?" When you get a *Yes* for the range, stop the pendant and start counting very, very slowly. Twenty-one, twenty-two, and so on until the pendant starts to move. Then confirm. If the pendant started to move on twenty-five, stop it and then ask, "Is it twenty-five?" You might get a *Yes* answer. If not, check for twenty-six, as the pendant may have just started to move for the next number.

Now that you get the picture, let's discuss locating missing animals. First secure a map of the area. Draw a horizontal line across the middle of the map, and an intersecting vertical line down the center. Hold the pendant over each quadrant formed by the lines, and ask, "Is he here?" You should get one Yes, and three No responses.

Draw the vertical and horizontal lines on your Yes quadrant and repeat the process. If you are using a map of a large area, you can change maps to show streets or smaller areas until you zero in on the location of the animal.

Remember, animals tend to move around, but many times I have found places where the animal has been sighted, using this method.

One of the strangest events I had with dowsing happened at a farm a mile from my home and involved BB, a horse you will be hearing more about later. She was nine weeks old and had almost weaned herself from her mother's milk, and had been eating grain and hay. The mares were eating laps of hay put out in the pasture and ignoring the grass that was starting to sprout all over. My horses at home were watching the grass sprouts push through the soil and grabbing them as soon as they appeared, so it did not seem to be a local problem.

I was asked to communicate with the horses at the farm to find out what was going on. BB let me know that her mother's milk did not taste good, and that her tongue felt like it had a nasty tasting coating on it. The other horses said the grass had been tasting bitter for days and was now even burning their mouths. They didn't seem to be able to tell me more than that.

Jean, the stable manager, felt that it might be helpful to consult a second animal communicator, which is what we decided to do. A call was placed to a second communicator who advised dowsing, and suggested that her father did a lot of dowsing, and he might tell us how to go about it. Since I had dowsed before, I was elected to do this job.

The instructions made sense and were easy to follow. I was told to give a gift to the grass and ask if I could communicate with it. I decided the gift to the grass would be whole wheat flour. I had recently learned about the Native American custom of returning something to the earth to leave it a better place than when you found it. Whole wheat flour came from a grass and was nourishing to us, so that felt right to me.

I fashioned a high-tech-coat-hanger-rod, and did use a Y shaped branch from a fruit tree as a back-up. I had respectfully asked the tree to help find the answers to the grass problem and snipped the branch as painlessly as possible.

I had a baggie of flour in one pocket, the Y branch from the tree in another, and my rods in my hands. My husband, Vic, was at my side with a pad of paper and a pen. Vic is my staunch supporter and reality checker. We entered the first of four pastures.

I did a brief meditation, sprinkled the wheat flour, and asked the three questions I had been instructed to ask:

- "May I ask questions?" (*permission*)
- "Can I ask questions?" (*do I have the ability*)
- "Should I ask questions?" (*was this the right thing to do*)

With each question the rods indicated a Yes answer, which delighted me.

Now was the time to ask the question about the grass problem. I asked whether the problem could be corrected, and got a *Yes*. Did the pastures need lime? *No*. Did they need any chemicals? *No*.

The process was long, with many questions asked and answered. I used both the rods and Y branch for the first dozen questions, and the answers were the same, so I finally used the rods for the rest. If I felt unsure I used the back-up branch.

This is where the story takes a strange twist. Jean had been using a homeopathic remedy on the horses. The rods had indicated that the pastures and paddocks should have drops from the bottle of that remedy put in certain places. All four pastures and all four paddocks were to be dowsed for the location and amount of drops. The locations were to be near the center of each area.

I walked to the approximate center of the first pasture and asked the rods if this was where the drops should go, and got a *Yes*. That seemed too easy, so I walked a few feet away and asked the same question. That time I got a *No*. I went back to the original place and got the original answer, *Yes*.

I sprinkled some of the flour on the ground to mark where the drops were to go, and went on to dowse the rest of the property. I used the Y branch once in a while just to double check, and the answers were always confirmed.

Jean arrived shortly after I completed this process. Together we walked the pastures and put the drops where they belonged, and then turned the horses out.

The horses began eating the grass at once, and within a week BB returned to mother's milk. The mare had almost dried up, but complied by making milk once more for her baby.

PART I

Collections

Dog Tales

The Stolen Guns

My friend Jean, who has worked for many years as a stable manager, had become quite good at communicating with animals. I had worked with her for a while, this gave us many opportunities to practice with the horses.

One day Jean's son, Larry, told her that his house had been burglarized, and several guns from his collection had been stolen. His next door neighbor had a daughter who had a bunch of boys hanging around her much of the time. At the time of the theft, her parents were out of state for a few days at a funeral. He asked Jean if she could talk to the neighbor's dog to see if it knew anything about the stolen guns.

Jean made mental contact with the dog, who told her that the guns were hidden under the girl's bed. Jean asked me to check, and I got the same message, plus that they were wrapped in an old tee shirt. The dog went on to give me a description of the boy who brought them into the house. The description included the blue striped shirt the boy was wearing. Larry asked another neighbor if he had seen any boys around that fit the description, and the neighbor confirmed the information.

Larry did not want to have problems with his neighbors, but he did want his guns back. One gun was an antique that had belonged to his great-grandfather. He had already called the police when he found the basement door broken in and the guns missing. There was not much the officer could do, other than file a report. If Larry called back and said that the dog had supplied him with information, he had a pretty good idea of the reception he would get.

He decided, instead, to stretch the truth. He called the officer and told him that he had received an anonymous message about the guns from a female. The dog was a female, so this wasn't too far off base. Larry gave the officer the details and asked if the police would go with him to talk to the girl's father to see if they could check under her bed.

When they approached the father with the story of the robbery, Larry explained that he did not want to make trouble, but he would like to check the information he had received. The father agreed, and wanted the police to question his daughter. He was disturbed by the company she was keeping and wanted her to see the problems that could arise.

Larry, the officer and the father checked under the bed, but the guns were not there. The officer questioned the teen, but she used an arrogant tone when she told them, "I don't know nothin."

After more questions she finally blurted out that she had been in school that Monday. Since Monday had not been mentioned, they knew they were on the right track, so the officer told her that they would check with the school to make sure she had been there. With this added pressure, she admitted that she had not, but did not know anything about the three stolen guns and three clips.

Larry was not aware that clips were missing, so he went home to check. They were gone. The girl was now realizing that she was in a bind, so she gave the names of the boys who had been at the house that day.

When the boys were questioned they said first that they were in the girl's house, but did not break in to Larry's. After telling a lot of lies and getting tripped up by them, they finally said they did it. Each of the three boys blamed the others. The guns had been taken to a nearby city and sold, so Larry's chances of ever getting his great-grandfather's gun back once again went down to zero.

The police pressed charges on the one boy who was eighteen, and he was found guilty and sent to jail. The other two got away free because of their ages.

Larry found out later that there had been another girl at the house that day, and wondered if the teens had tried to find out who made the anonymous phone call. If they all denied it they would have been telling the truth - for once.

Post Script...*eight months later* - Larry's great-grandfather's gun was found in Philadelphia. Since the robbery report was listed in the police files, they were able to easily trace its rightful owner. Although the serial numbers had been painted black, that is a repair that can be easily handled. Great-grandfather was obviously not going to let his heirloom out of the family for very long!

A Well Informed Dog

Betsey Karl made an appointment for a consultation to talk to her black sheep dog, Kelly. Kelly had just been diagnosed with lymphoma cancer, and Betsey wanted to know if she was in any pain and what treatments she wanted.

Kelly was very matter-of-fact about her condition. She told me she did not hurt unless the swelling was pressed, and then she mentioned chemotherapy. Betsey confirmed the information that Kelly was scheduled to see the veterinarian the next day. Kelly told me that there was a kind of chemo that would not make her sick, and that is what she wanted. This surprised me somewhat since I had not heard of anything like that for animals. I kiddingly asked Betsey if Kelly had been reading the newspapers or magazines. Betsy said she did not think so, but she had explained all the options to Kelly, including the type of chemo that Kelly told me about.

The next question was painful to ask, but Betsey managed well. Suppose the chemo did not do the job, how long did Kelly want to hold out? Again, Kelly was pragmatic. If her bladder or bowels became a problem, she did not want to put Betsey, or herself, through an ordeal. She was a proud dog and wanted to retain her dignity. She also requested that Betsey periodically check in to see if Kelly felt things were going according to her wishes. Betsey promised she would do that.

The Biopsy

A call came in about a dog who had a needle biopsy for liver cancer. The results were not conclusive enough for the owner and she wanted a surgical biopsy. The dog was angry and said, "You want to see a liver? I'll show you a liver!" I instantly had a picture in my mind of a liver colored pancake with small bubbles all over it. The dog said, "When the bubbles leak I feel sick." I asked him if he had tumors. He said he did not, just bubbles.

The owner verified that the veterinarian had described the cancer exactly the same way, and that the seepage made the dog feel ill. The owner then asked the dog if she should still order the biopsy.

The angry voice of the dog filled my head with the words, "I TOLD YOU what the liver looks like."

She decided against the biopsy, and she and the dog decided to use homeopathic remedies to fight the cancer.

Think Yellow

Basil is an English Bull Dog. He is quite proud of his ferocious looks because he can be as sweet as he wants, but still instill fear in the heart of anyone who would want to hurt Marlene.

When Marlene called and described Basil my teeth began to hurt, so I asked if he had a dental problem. She said he did not, but he had just had his teeth scaled the day before at the veterinarian's. That was what I was feeling from him. We talked about a few minor physical things that were going on with him, and then went on to the reason Marlene had called.

Marlene wanted to know how Basil would feel if she brought another dog into the house to keep him company. There was a short pause, and then Basil said, "I don't want a puppy. I would like to have a dog who is at least a year old."

Marlene said, "Do you want to hear something weird?" I laughed. If you have gotten this far in this book you must know that I hear things every day that are considered *weird* by most people. I have come to consider the so-called *weird* statements pretty normal. Never routine, but normal.

She went on to tell me that the companion she and her husband were considering for Basil was a little female, one-and-a-half years old. Marlene had explained everything to Basil, but she was not sure he understood. He did.

Marlene also wanted to let Basil know that she was going to be away for a week, but that she would be back. Did he understand?

He said that he did understand, and that he had a message. He told me that the color yellow was very special. Marlene confirmed it was her favorite, and to her represented happiness.

Basil said it was more than that, and there was something yellow that was important to both of them. Marlene thought a minute, and then realized that it was her old bathrobe that Basil slept on. He said that was the color, and when she was away and wanted him to know she was thinking about him, she was to bring the yellow color of the bathrobe into her mind. He would do the same, so if she had the color fill her mind it was because he was telling her that all was well with him.

Marlene agreed to do as he asked, and told me she felt much easier about leaving Basil for the week.

While away on her trip, Marlene woke early each morning to have quiet meditation and commune with Basil. One morning she awoke late and missed the meditation time. When she called home later in the day, her husband told her that everything was fine, but Basil seemed upset. Marlene realized that he had missed her meditation/communication time. The rest of the trip they communicated and all went well.

A Gift From Sox

Sox was delightful to talk to, as was his person, Jane, who lived close to us in Pennsylvania. When Sox had answered all of Jane's questions, and we were about to end the consultation, Jane asked one more question: "Does Sox have anything he would like to tell me?"

Sox immediately responded with, "More meat." I asked Jane if she was a vegetarian, and she said "Yes." She kept Sox on a vegetarian diet, too. She said she had no trouble giving Sox meat sometimes, and would take care of getting him some at once.

When I opened my mail a few days later there was a check from Jane. The envelope held a special treat for me. There was a note from Sox. The letters were cut out of a magazine, it said:

> Dear Anita,
> More Meat!
> Bliss in Bechtlesville
> Some things get better with age. Thanks for understanding.
> Love, Sox

There was a five dollar bill clipped onto the letter. I have the letter and the money framed and hanging in my office.

I did send Sox a thank you note and offered my computer and typing skills any time he needed to send someone else a letter.

TV Star?

Donna Blagdan Kuchter scheduled a consultation about her German Shepherd, Dax. As soon as she told me his name and breed my neck started to hurt. I told her about his neck, and asked why she had called. Donna said she was calling because she felt Dax had a neck problem, but the veterinarians had not been able to find anything. We discussed that situation a bit more. Donna felt with more information Dax's veterinarian would now be able to help.

The next question Donna had was about Dax's training - did he like his work? The prompt response was, "Oh yes, I crouch down."

I didn't know what kind of training program he was in, so I asked Donna if that was right. She said that he was training for obedience and protection, and doing quite well, except for being a bit too exuberant at times. Dax said he loved the training.

Donna and I discussed the problem that Dax was too rough with their other dogs. Dax said he would like to have a big dog to play with; one that he could throw around and could also throw him around. Dax said that being thrown was "the best fun."

Donna laughed and told me that she never saw a dog that loved to be thrown. Her husband and Dax played all the time. Donna's husband would throw Dax, and he would bounce up immediately and run back for more. (I'm sure it was done safely, and Dax assured me that it was not why his neck hurt.)

Dax then told me he was going to be on television. I asked Donna if she had any plans to have him on a television program, and she responded with a surprised "No."

Dax repeated that he was going to be on television. Donna suddenly remembered that she and her husband had videotaped Dax as he moved around so they could show the veterinarian. Dax had associated being videoed with being on TV, since that was the playback method.

The Golden Benninghoff's

Thirteen years ago, when Todd Benninghoff was graduating from high school, his parents purchased Mariah, a bouncy Golden Retriever bitch. Todd and Mariah spent many happy years together. When Todd married and moved out of state, Mariah remained in the family home.

Eleven years ago, Mariah had a litter of pups that the family had planned to sell. Well, that isn't exactly the way it turned out. Travis became Gloria's companion (Todd's mother). Isiah, Biancia and Simone also remained within the family. Recently a newcomer has been added. Brady was introduced to the house full of now elderly dogs. This could have presented a problem, since Brady is a perpetual bundle of energy, but no one seems to mind. Brady dances for his breakfast and bows when he is fed. The other dogs look after him with loving patience.

Gloria Bennignhoff decided she wanted to have a consultation on the state of all of the family pets, so we began an interesting appointment. We started with Isiah. Gloria wanted to know if Isiah wanted to go and live with Todd, even though Todd and his wife had gotten another dog. She wanted Isiah to be happy, even if it meant breaking up the dog family.

As soon as I made contact with Isiah I asked Gloria what was wrong with his face. I could feel a strong pull on the entire left side of my face. Since this was our first consultation, Gloria gasped with surprise that I was able to pick this up. She told me that Isiah had cancer which resulted in his having the right side of his jaw removed. The sensation that I felt was gravity pulling at the left side due to the missing jaw and reconstruction of his face.

Isiah was quick to tell me that he did not mind the changes in his face or the fact that his tongue hung out most of the time. He said he felt very special because he was fed canned food and it was cut up for him. He told me, "They would chew it for me if they thought I needed it."

Isiah was quite willing to discuss Todd and his future. He said he had spent a lot of time just being still and thinking. Gloria confirmed that he had been doing that lately.

Isiah said that he had bonded with Todd at birth, but now he knew that Gloria was the one who needed him. His next statement was bittersweet: "I always want to live here, but Todd is my heaven."

Gloria asked if Isiah knew how much she loved him. Isiah answered with a question, "Does she know how much I love her? I would die for her." I had heard several other pets say the same thing to their loved ones, and it never ceased to bring tears to my eyes.

Our next conversation was with Travis who quickly let me know he had pains in his neck and ribs. (Gloria later made an appointment to take Travis to a veterinarian who incorporates chiropractic and acupuncture with her treatment program. The doctor confirmed the neck problem, and appropriate care was instituted.)

This out of the way, Travis said he wanted to discuss another family Golden. Gloria asked if that was Brady. Travis quickly responded "Yes."

He continued, "I want to be like an uncle to Brady, and teach him the rules. In order to do this I would request that the family not call me *Travvie* in front of Brady. It is not dignified and if I am to be the teacher, I need to be respected." Gloria said she would be happy to pass this along to the family and would be happy to see Travis fulfill this roll.

Simone was next on the conversation list. When I started to talk to her I felt *spaced out*. I asked Gloria if Simone was on any medication, and found out that she has a thyroid problem. Her doctor has described her condition as feeling like someone who wakes up with a hangover.

Simone said she is the watch dog of the group. She usually chooses to just lay around and watch the other dogs at play. Occasionally she will briefly join in the fun, but is mostly content watching. Simone assured me that she is "very happy with my position and role in the family."

Jancie, Todd's sister, wanted to talk to Bianca. She was concerned about Bianca's understanding of why Brady was with them. Apparently her concern was valid. Bianca thought Brady, who she always referred to as "The Baby," was there to replace her, and wondered what she had done wrong. She had been depressed for some time.

Jancie had told Bianca from the beginning, "Brady is not here to replace you." The problem with this statement is that there is no *picture* for the negative words, such as 'not,' 'don't,' 'can't,' and so on. Bianca only pictured *the Baby* replacing her, and was so relieved to hear Jancie tell her that she was still her number one dog. Jancie explained that Brady had been purchased as her dog because she wanted a dog to show. That would be Brady's job. (Jancie told me later that Bianca's depression lifted that day and has not returned.)

Bianca wanted to give Jancie some messages. She said she loved the song that Jancie sang to her that "goes up and down." Jancie laughed and explained she made up a silly song and always sang it to Bianca. It was a bouncy tune.

Bianca said she always waited at the door to go bye-bye and get ice cream. Jancie confirmed that this was their *special treat.* Bianca was mellow when she said, "You always tell me that you love me."

Bianca went on to describe pains in her shoulders, back, and chest, and difficulty breathing, a situation that is not unusual in older large dogs. (This was also confirmed by the veterinarian and treatments to ease the conditions were provided.)

Jancie said that she fears the time when Bianca will leave her, and does not know how she will ever deal with losing her. Bianca answered, "I'll always be with you in the room where the windows open out."

That room is the Benninghoff kitchen. Jancie sits in the kitchen with Bianca when she comes home late from her nursing shift at the hospital and the rest of the family is asleep. It is always a special time for both of them, and always will be.

This concluded the consultation as there were no questions for Brady, the puppy. Brady did not mind, he didn't have anything to say anyway.

It's Not Always Clear Sailing!

Sometimes my animal communications conversations are received with skepticism. This can be painful for me since I so sincerely believe in all my animal friends and appreciate the openness with which they greet me.

I called a young woman who had left a message on my machine. She told me the name of a person who had given her my number and told me her dog had a tumor. As soon as she said that I began to have an ache on my left side in the lower abdominal area.

I asked to confirm if that was the location of the tumor. She could not contain the shock she felt, and cried, "How do you do that?"

She excitedly told her mother what had happened, and her mother picked up the extension to join the conversation. We talked a bit about animal communications, and then the mother asked if I did "hands-on healing." I told her I practiced Reiki and am a Reiki Master, but not as part of my animal communication occupation.

I learned Reiki to deepen my work with communications, and to do it for my friends and family, but if they were interested in pursuing this modality for their dog, I could supply them with names of individuals who practice Reiki on animals. Although they did not seem satisfied with that, I did give them some practioneers' numbers.

They then asked when I could see the dog to communicate. I told them I work by telephone and would be happy to schedule an appointment. That statement was met with disbelief. I don't find that response unusual, so I explained, in a little more detail, how I work.

The mother was not convinced that I could know how the dog felt if I did not "look in its eyes." I did not remind her that I had just told her where the dog's tumor was, but instead, told her that if she was uncomfortable not to make an appointment. I could understand how she felt.

The daughter wanted to make the appointment. She worked in the field of social services, and her mind was oriented more toward science, but she had heard how accurate I was with her friend's dog. She felt she was open-minded enough to pursue a consultation, so we arranged a convenient time.

When the call came in at the appointed time, the mother and daughter were both on the phone. I asked the usual question: "Please tell me the name of the dog and a brief physical description." As the daughter started to talk I felt the pressure of the tumor once again. I told her she could stop, and concentrated on what the dog was sending me.

I described the problem in both hind legs, but the left was worse, and the daughter confirmed that the dog had arthritis, and had been given shots of cortisone at one time for the situation.

The dog did not show me any signs of pain along the spine or in the neck, and I told them that. My hands began to hurt then. My knuckles felt swollen and inflamed, and I just wanted to rub them and keep them warm. I had seen people with arthritis do that with their hands, so passed that information on. The daughter said they thought there was a problem with the dog's pads, and I responded that I believed it to be the joints in the paws. At that point I just knew that the dog licked her paws to try to heal the sore joints. I told them that she licked her paws a lot, and that was confirmed.

At this point the mother asked her first question: "What is her favorite toy?" I got the answer in the form of a word, not a picture. "Ball."

I said that she told me it was a ball.

The mother said, "What color?"

I told her I had not seen the ball and I usually think of a dog's toy ball as a pink rubber one, but I did not know.

The mother shot back, "No it's not pink. What does she like to do with the ball?"

I got nothing from the dog, and told the mother that I did not know.

The mother was not willing to let her line of questioning go, she persevered with asking who the dog loved best. I was starting to shut down. The dog had been giving me accurate information about her health, and that was all the dog wanted to discuss.

I tried to steer the conversation back to the tumor and treatments they were considering. The dog said she wanted to recover and was willing to undergo surgery and chemotherapy if that would help. However, if the family wanted to try alternative treatments she was open to that, too. It was to be their choice, and she would do her best to get better.

The daughter said she was surprised that the dog felt that way, as she usually had strong opinions on most matters. The dog confirmed that she was willing to try what ever they wanted, and did not mind which it was.

The mother's voice came back on the line, "What about the rest of the family? There are more in this family than just the two of us. Have her tell you who else is in the family."

At that point I felt that I had supplied enough information for them to know that I was in contact with their dog, and I did not have to perform any *tricks* to prove myself.

The feeling of negativity had become so strong that I could not cut through it to keep talking to the dog. I told them both that I could get no more, and this was the end of the conversation. If they had strong doubts and suspicions that was up to them, and there would be no charge for the time I had spent. I wished them luck with the dog.

The daughter, who continued to remain very reasonable, said she had one more question. She understood the feeling I was getting, and she had felt the negativity, too, but would I just tell her if there was anything wrong in the dog's mouth.

I said there was, on the upper left side. She said the dog had been treated for an abscess there. Was it completely healed?

I told her the dog said there was still a problem, and to take it up with the veterinarian. Actually, I was surprised that the dog popped back into my head, but then I realized that the abscess was still bothering her and she wanted it taken care of. She was a sweet, intelligent dog, and I was glad I could still do something for her.

The daughter said she still wanted to pay for the consultation since it had been helpful, and perhaps she would call again.

After this call I took some time to sit and meditate, and get in touch with my feelings about being tested. It actually happens quite often. The animals are usually quite willing to supply information that tells the person the message is truly coming from them.

As I contemplated the human distrust issue, I was able to understand that what finally felt soothing was the knowledge that **I am here to help the animals.** Whatever I can do, I must. Even though some people question animal communications, that is not my concern. It is the animals who have not been able to be heard. Through me and many others like me who have become dedicated to animal communications, they now have a voice.

It is my deep love and respect of animals that is my motivation to continue to communicate with them.

The Pulsing Energy

One winter Suzanne Warfield was having a problem with her Pomeranian, Stanley. Stanley had been barking, for days, in the sun room that had been added on to the house. He fixed his gaze at a corner where the wall met the ceiling, and barked and barked and barked. They lived in an old farm house, so Suzanne's husband joked that Stanley was barking at a ghost. Suzanne scheduled an appointment with me so I could ask Stanley what was going on.

When I asked Stanley, he told me there was energy in the corner that was "pulsing." Suzanne asked if it had been going on for a long time, and Stanley said that it had started recently.

Suzanne asked me to wait while she went to where Stanley did his barking. She wanted to see if she could see anything that could cause pulsing energy. She did. There was a rain gutter outside that had heat tape wrapped around it to keep it from freezing. It seemed that Stanley could hear the thermostatically controlled tape as it turned on and off, so he barked at it. Suzanne told Stanley that he was a silly dog, barking at heat tape. Stanley was satisfied and stopped his barking.

Mrs. Miller's Dog

Mrs. Miller is a teacher at an agriculture school. There are many animals at the school, and Mrs. Miller adds a few by bringing her dogs to class with her. I was asked to speak about animal communications to the students one day. The teenagers listened politely, and asked some questions. One boy stood up and said, "If you can really do this, tell Mrs. Miller's dog to go over to her side," as he pointed to the sleeping German Shepherd.

I explained that I would not *tell* the dog anything, but I would *ask* her to go. I reminded the student that a request is sometimes answered with a "No."

The young man stood his ground, and said, "Go ahead, tell her!" Had he even heard me?

I called the dog's name softly, she woke up and looked at me. I asked her if she would be so kind as to go and stand beside Mrs. Miller, and then go back and resume her nap. As I spoke I made sure I was forming clear images of what I wanted in my mind.

She looked at me for a few seconds, yawned, and slowly stood. The sweet dog walked over to Mrs. Miller, turned and looked at the students, and then walked back to her mat to lay down.

For a few seconds you could have heard a pin drop, then came the first, "Wow!" The students were so excited that their chatter even woke the one who had glared at me when I started my talk, and then fell asleep with his head cradled in his arms on the desk.

While they were talking to each other I whispered to Mrs. Miller, "Buy the darling any treat she wants and send me the bill." It is not unusual for an animal to do what this dog had just done, but she had just saved the day for me!

Cat Connections

When I have asked cats to describe a person I have almost always found that they start at the feet. I suppose that is the part of the person that they see first. I have watched my cats, and sure enough, they usually look at my feet as they greet me. I found this to be true, also, in the following stories.

The Thief

A girl called me to talk to her horses before she left for school for three months. Between the time she called to make the appointment, and the actual appointment time, some money was stolen from her room. So this being the urgent matter, this is where we began.

Since Petunia, the young lady's cat, was home at the time of the incident, she thought she might be able to be of help. I was given a description of the cat and Petunia was more than happy to be of assistance.

When I asked if she had any idea who might have been involved, Petunia showed me images of a pair of brown shoes, and a pair of dark sneakers. The girl said the brown shoes were hers. The cat agreed.

It once again showed me an image of dark-colored, high-top sneakers. A few seconds later I saw hairy men's legs. After another few seconds lag, denim cutoff shorts came into view. Finally, after a dark shirt, I could see a young man with dark hair, but the features were not clear to me. It was okay because by now the girl knew who the person was.

She asked if the individual stopped to pet the cat. Petunia responded that she had hidden under the bed, and showed me a bed with a light bedspread on it. The girl said her bedspread was white, and that was where the cat always ran to hide.

I could then see the feet and legs as the person walked to where the cat showed me a dresser, and the girl confirmed that the dresser was there, and that's where the money had been located. The cat said the person did not go anywhere else in the room, and left quickly. It was confirmed that nothing else was missing. I never heard whether the girl ever got her money back, but she obviously knew the person Petunia described.

The Cat Shooter

An elderly gentleman, who lived in a tiny rural town, called to arrange an emergency appointment to discuss his cat. The cat came home bloody and hurt. When the veterinarian saw the cat, he quickly identified that it had been shot in the face. The cat's jaw was damaged and he had lost a couple of teeth. The man wanted to know who would do such a thing.

The cat started at the feet, and sent me a picture of laced boots that were a brown color, and muddy. As he scanned upward I saw blue jeans, then a tee shirt, and finally the face of a boy in his early teens. The boy had black hair.

The man asked if the cat heard a loud noise before he felt the pain, and the cat said there was a noise, but it was not loud. His description sounded more like an air gun than a rifle.

The man set about to do some detective work, but did not feel he could tell anyone that his cat had supplied a description of the culprit. He called me several days later to tell me he knew who it was.

There was a young teenager who came to the little town to visit his divorced father. He had the clothes the cat had described, but they are common teenage garb. The distinction was the boy fit the physical description supplied by the cat. He also had an air gun, and had a reputation of going around shooting cats. The owner of the cat said he was not going to retaliate, or do anything unlawful, but wanted to thank me for my help and that he would now handle the situation. I didn't ask any more information about what his plans were, I'm not sure I want to know.

Puddy Finds A New Litter Box

Puddy had used her litter box for years without any problems. One day she stopped using the box and started to consider the fireplace her special commode. When Nancy Cava, Puddy's human companion, made an appointment to ask me talk to Puddy, I could hear the desperation in her voice. Nancy's husband, Joe, was too angry to think of anything but getting rid of Puddy.

The story goes that when you walked in the front door of their home it was quite obvious that Puddy had relieved herself in the ashes. Manufacturers of kitty litter go to great lengths to make a product that will disguise the typical cat litter aroma. Ashes do not act as a cover-up. I was Puddy's last chance of keeping her comfortable home.

As soon as I contacted Puddy, the tips of my fingers felt numb and tingly. It was very much like the feeling one gets at the dentist office when the Novocain is almost worn off. I asked if Puddy had been declawed, and found that she had. Then I asked if Nancy had changed the brand of litter she used, possibly to a coarser type. Again, the answer was "Yes."

Puddy still felt the effects of her declawing years after it had been done. She did not like the feel of the coarse litter on her tender paws, so she looked for a place that would feel softer. The ashes in the fireplace were perfect.

Nancy changed litter brands and Puddy went back to the litter box immediately.

Joe was still not convinced that the cat should stay. However, soon after this incident, when he was recuperating from a long serious illness, it was Puddy who curled up in his lap and purred every day. Now they're good pals.

Take One Cat And Call Me In The Morning...

In 1995 my husband, Vic, had a painful back problem. Each night when Vic settled into bed our cat, Seven, would jump onto the bed, put his nose against Vic's for a brief touch, and then inspect Vic's back. He walked up and down beside Vic and checked until he reached the most painful area. He would then lay down with his body against the sore back, and go to sleep for the night. When Vic woke each morning the part of his back that the cat slept against was the least painful.

Medical Thoughts

I will never tell anyone what medicines to give their animals, nor will I suggest changes. I do, however, tell the person how the animal says he feels on the medication he is receiving. One horse told me he wanted the medicine "in the water." I didn't know what the horse meant, but the owner said it was electrolytes, but the horse would not drink the water with them in it. Apparently the horse had changed his mind, because when she again offered the water with electrolytes, the horse drank it.

The following two calls came in about a month apart:

Annika Saracini's cat, Melanie, was sick. When asked what would make her feel better, Melanie told me about a brown liquid in a dropper bottle. In the picture she sent me the liquid looked like gravy. When I told Annika that she knew at once what it was since she took vitamins from a dropper bottle, and it looks like gravy.

Melanie said that was what she wanted. When Annika understood that the cat realized that the vitamins Annika was taking helped her to feel good, the cat wanted some of that same energy.

About a month later Phyllis Rice called about her cat, Baby, who had pneumonia. She was not responding to drugs. Again the cat requested medicine that came in a dropper bottle. Phyllis said she knew what it was; the cat had been on penicillin before and it had helped.

The cat went on to say that she also wanted some other natural medicine, which she described. I mentioned that the formula sounded like one that could be found in a book, *Natural Health for Dogs and Cats*. When we looked up the formula it was the correct treatment for the disease the cat had.

Phyllis checked with the veterinarian, changed medications, and the cat got better. The wisdom of animals never ceases to amaze me.

Winchester's Message

When Margo Woodacre called it was just before the end of this lifetime for Winchester. He had been the family animal companion for over a decade and felt he had a long and happy life. Margo and her family were quite upset about losing him and heard about animal communications. Margo asked if I could tell Winchester how loved he was before he left them.

Winchester was always happy to hear how much his family loved him, and welcomed the opportunity to respond by letting them know that he loved them too, and asked me to "tell the big fella not to worry." Margo told me that her husband was very tall, and always referred to Winchester as "the old fella."

Margo sent this letter in the hope that it might help comfort others with their losses:

"Winchester was our loyal, loving, one-eyed, fourteen year old cat. We took him in as a stray when he was a young adult. We knew that he had an exciting life...lost an eye, broke his pelvis, left us twice, but always returned...if only he could write his stories! No matter what the challenge, Winchester would always bounce back. He was one wise, old cat.

"Last August, however, Winchester stopped eating. He was not well and the many hospital stays did little to help him. Sad as it was for us to admit, we all felt that he was ready to move on.

"On Winchester's last day in this world, I had a long loving conversation with him and asked him when he passed over, if possible, to send a message to us to tell us that he was fine. And just as I sat with him in the silence of our study, our favorite mocking bird landed on our chimney (as he often did during the spring) and began singing his many beautiful songs. I asked Winchester to send whatever message he wished but if he wanted to send the mockingbird to sing that would be fine.

"That evening we had him put to sleep. My husband, daughter and I felt lost and deeply saddened. Needless to say, both my husband and I had an emotional and sleepless night. At about 5:00 a.m., we began talking about how much we missed our 'old fella' and the tears began to fall. Suddenly in the stillness and darkness of the early morning, came the beautiful songs of our favorite bird. He had landed on the bedroom chimney and his voice echoed down the shaft sounding vibrant! The bird had never done this in the darkness of early morning...the sun was more than an hour from rising! Both Ernie and I held each other and smiled...suddenly we were at peace...our message was sent! Our wise, old cat, once again, bounced back as he always did!

"The bird returned for the rest of that week and sang from our bedroom chimney each morning after sun-up. This was such a happy reminder of our *special fella* and, very importantly, a reminder that life is everlasting."

Horse Stories

Dog, Cat and Rollo (the horse)

You might think there is a mistake because of the **Horse Stories** heading on this chapter, and it starts with a dog (and cat) story. It's okay, keep reading.

We have a cat named Seven. We had run out of cat names, and gone to the numbering system. We asked him if we could name him Seven, and got his approval. My husband calls all cats Tibby, so Seven actually has two names, but he said he doesn't mind.

Seven came to us when our lovely dog, Puppy was quite ill. Seven said his purpose was to help Puppy through her transition when she moved on through this journey to another plane. Seven did a wonderful job in helping by alerting us several times when Puppy was ill, and was company for her when we were out during the day.

After Puppy passed away, Seven was at the age to be neutered. I did not want to upset him, so I wordlessly whisked him up one day and took him to the veterinarian to have the deed done. He came home the next day, and it was clear that he was furious with me. That was understandable, but the anger went on for two weeks. Finally, one day I sat down with him and asked why he was still so angry with me.

Seven let me know in no uncertain terms, that I, who could communicate with animals, should have let him know what was going to happen. When he went to the veterinarian's he thought his job had been finished and we were going to euthanize him. He was not ready to leave this life, and was frightened and upset. If I had explained, he would have understood. I apologized and promised him I would always tell him what was going to happen to him in the future.

I told my friend, Linda Briel, the story and she asked me to tell her young stallion, Rollo, that he was going to be castrated in a few days. I dropped by their home the next day and Linda and I went into the barn to talk to Rollo.

Rollo was tied in the stall waiting for me. He had an empty plastic milk bottle hanging from a beam, and was hitting it with his nose. He would then bite the rope that tied him, and then swing over to bite his rubber feed bucket. I greeted him and asked if I could talk to him.

The answer came, "Okay, talk. Play with the toy, bite the rope, bite the bucket. Play with the toy, bite the rope, bite the bucket."

I asked him to please listen because I wanted him to know the veterinarian was coming the next day. Now I heard, "Okay, talk, the veterinarian's coming. Play with the toy, bite the rope, bite the bucket." He just kept repeating in kind of a singsong cadence, in spite of my efforts.

I got tired of the game, and flashed him a picture of him laying on the ground. One person was across his neck, pinning him to the ground, another held his leg up, and the third was the veterinarian carving him.

He said, "Play with the toy, bite the...What!?! Why would they do that to me?"

Linda and I had to laugh. He had stopped playing so suddenly, and stared into my eyes. His ears were so far forward as he concentrated that I thought they were going to cross. However, I did have his undivided attention at this point.

Rollo first wanted to know "Why?" I explained that if he remained a stallion hormones would rule his life. He was already starting to nip at people, and was difficult to lead, in spite of being reprimanded. Stallions are usually dangerous around women and girls. Linda and her daughter would always have to worry around him. He said he would stop biting, and he was sure he could control himself around Linda and her daughter. Well...pretty sure.

I went on to explain that he would seldom be used as a breeding stallion. Also, he had said that he wanted to be a show horse and stallions were not desirable in the classes he would be shown in.

Rollo never took his eyes off of me as he considered what I had said. Then he asked, "Will it hurt?" There were some more questions and I gave the best answers I could. When he felt satisfied that he had all the information he needed, he said he would not fight it. I promised I would be there with him when the veterinarian came in case he had any more questions.

When the veterinarian arrived Linda introduced me, and told him I was an animal communicator. He smiled and said he hoped I had not told the horse what was going to happen to him on this day. I just smiled, but didn't answer. Many veterinarians are strong supporters of animal communicators and invite the opportunity to work in conjunction with each other. Other times you know to just stand back and be there for the animal.

When the veterinarian finished, he said it was one of the easiest castrations he had done. Rollo was as good as gold, even when the veterinarian had trouble finding a vein to tranquilize him, and had to poke around with the needle Rollo just stood and waited. Animals as well as humans welcome the opportunity to be informed as to what to expect with a new experience.

Brownie

I was at Sandy's farm with her and Brownie's rider. The rider was a college girl who rode Brownie on the trail and in shows. Brownie is one of the biggest horses I have ever seen. He is a Tennessee Walker, a proud horse with an enormous head. Even with his size, Brownie is extremely gentle.

Sandy asked what Brownie liked about living with her, and he immediately replied, "The singing."

Sandy said I was wrong because she had an awful voice and never sang - even if she was alone. The rider said that she sang when she rode. I could see a mental picture of the horse swinging his head, and hear the tune of *This Old Man*. That was the song she sang as she rode.

Sandy asked Brownie what he did not like and he said there was a loud whistle that went off at regular intervals. We were high in the hills and there were no factories around to have such a whistle, so I was sure I was mistaken. After some questioning we realized that it was the siren at the fire company, just over the hill, that went off every Saturday at noon.

Brownie was asked what he did not like about his rider's skills. He indicated that when she mounted, and before she sat in the saddle, she stood in the saddle and wiggled her butt back and forth. She acknowledged that she did. He told her to "Stop."

I had been called to speak to Brownie because he took long strides with his front legs, and short choppy ones with his hind legs. He could never win a ribbon in a show. There had been two veterinarians who had pronounced him sound, two horseshoers who could not help, and several trainers who could do nothing about his gait.

I asked Brownie to mentally show me where his front hooves were, and he did. I asked him to show me where his chest was, and again he did. When I asked where his hind hooves were he showed me a picture of a very short-bodied horse with hind feet only a few inches behind the front ones. Actually he was a huge horse with a long body, but his view of himself was distorted.

I suggested tying a rope from his neck to his back end, and around his rump so he could feel his body. I was there on a Thursday, and got a call on Monday that Brownie had been in a show the day before and received four ribbons. He won the Hunter Under Saddle, an award that is judged on the way the horse moves.

L' Girl

Wanda was frantic when she left a message on my answering machine one morning. Her Morgan mare, L' Girl had been ill for two days. She seemed to have colic the first day, and the veterinarian had treated her, but the next day she was still breaking out in a sweat at times and trying to lay down in her stall.

Wanda, the barn staff, and a friend were taking turns keeping L' Girl on her feet. The veterinarian had suggested that she be taken to a large animal hospital and be examined for an ulcer since this was going on too long to be an ordinary case of colic.

I did not get the message until about seven in the evening, but I had met L' Girl a few times, and was able to connect with her before I returned Wanda's call. I was a bit surprised to find that L' Girl did not have pain where I usually feel it when an animal has colic, and certainly not where I would think an ulcer would hurt, but instead it was in the area of an ovary. The surprise continued when I asked her what caused the pain and she told me, "The dark pellets I eat." Maybe it was colic, after all.

Since this was an emergency situation, I didn't hesitate, but called the barn as Wanda sounded distraught. I asked what L' Girl was being fed, and it was barley, oats, and corn. No pellets there. She did get a pelleted vitamin supplement, but the pellets were a light color. Then Wanda remembered that L' Girl was getting thyroid medicine every day that did not taste good. It was given to her in sweet feed, which has dark pellets in it. L' Girl did not know there was medicine in the feed, but she thought that eating the feed made her sick. She also told me she was in her heat cycle, which Wanda confirmed.

When we talked about L' Girl being in heat, someone remembered that the veterinarian had palpated L' Girl during the examination, and when she was near the right ovary L' Girl shot forward. It was starting to sound like L' Girl was having menstrual cramps, not colic or an ulcer.

Animal communication is not a replacement for veterinary care, and I do not like to contradict the veterinarians, so I suggested that Wanda might ask the veterinarian some questions about the possibility of her pain being connected to her cycle.

Immediately after our conversation, Wanda contacted her veterinarian and relayed the messages. Although somewhat skeptical as to the source, the veterinarian agreed that the scenario was certainly possible. The veterinarian worked out a change in L' Girl's thyroid medication and Wanda had L' Girl massaged with a combination of equine massage and Shiatsu. Later that evening a much happier horse was grazing in the pasture and feeling fine.

Horseshoers

Proper nutrition, veterinary care and exercise are essential in animal care. Additionally, in the world of horses, the farrier (horseshoer) can make the difference between winning or losing a race or competition...or just having comfortable feet to stand around on. After all, horses spend most of their life on their feet. Being comfortable with the shoes they are wearing is critical.

Any number of things can go wrong with a horse's hooves which will cause him to be laid up for an entire season. I don't know if there is a master plan, but if a horse is going to lose a shoe, it is usually just before the day of a show. If your horse pulls up lame each time he is shod, this can be a disaster. A horseshoer you can trust to do the right job and one who is there as scheduled, is a person you respect.

These are three stories of some lovely people I have worked with.

Tim Phillips

Horseshoers find my service invaluable at times, and when I find one who believes in what I do, and wants to learn, I am happy to teach him or her. Tim Phillips takes care of my horses' hooves. Tim believed in animal communication from the first time I met him, and I was grateful, so I offered to teach him how I communicate. He learned how to send images to an unruly horse immediately, and was able to *slide into the horse's body* the first time he tried. From that vantage point, the horseshoer can realize if the angle of the hoof is correct, if there is pain, or if other problems may exist. Although much of that is already done by an experienced horseshoer as he works, communicating is a great back-up and confirmation of the work.

Tim had a chance to use communications very soon after his lesson on sending images. He was the horseshoer at a competitive trail ride. One of the horses threw a shoe, and Tim was asked to nail it back on. The rider told Tim that the horse was unruly when it was being shod and he would try to keep it calm, but it would not be easy.

Before Tim started to work on the horse he told it what he was going to do and that everything would go quickly if the horse stood quietly. Much to the surprise of the rider, the horse stood very still until Tim was finished.

Tim was the last horseshoer to trim the hooves of our pony, Sally, before she died. At that time, Sally was about thirty-four years old, she had arthritis, and could only stand for a short time before she would have pain. I held her for Tim as he worked. When Sally started to hurt, I told Tim where and what kind of pain she had. Sometimes it was a cramp, and sometimes it was the searing burn of the arthritis. Tim would adjust the position of her leg, or put her foot down if that was needed. He only held her little hoof a few inches off the ground to work, and I was glad I was not putting myself into *his* body to feel how his back must have ached.

Sally got through the trimming of her hooves better than she had in years. Since it turned out to be her final trim, I was even more grateful.

Jack Phoebus

I met Jack at Dr. Judith Shoemaker's clinic one day when I went to visit with a couple of friends. Judith was going to be busy for a few minutes and requested that we go and look at the horse in the blacksmith area, but be extra careful around this horse. Due to neurological problems, the horse was quite dangerous for the farrier to work on. This was why Judith had requested that we be present in case Jack would have any trouble.

The horse was for sale, with an asking price of over six hundred thousand dollars. He was on his way back home to California after winning championships in several major east coast shows. My friends and I were interested in seeing what a horse that valuable looked like close up, so we were happy to be of assistance and hustled off to see him.

We went in and stood quietly, as Jack was holding the horse's leg up. At this point in the shoeing, Jack was directly under the horse. Now, this is a dangerous place to be, no matter what horse you are working on. If the horse is startled, it will generally kick and you have no place to go.

Jack looked up and saw us. He immediately told us to stand back, as this horse was very unpredictable and when he blew up it was an ugly scene. The three of us stood well away and made sure there was an escape route handy in case we had to run.

My friend Susan, the most outgoing member of our group, introduced herself to Jack and told him that Judith had suggested that we come, look at the horse, and remain to be of any help if needed. Jack greeted us while continuing with his work.

I, generally quite shy and usually the *wallflower* in a group situation, chimed in with, "Hi, my name is Anita Curtis." To my surprise, Jack put the horse's hoof down and came over to shake my hand, telling me that he had wanted to meet me for some time. He told me I could stand anywhere I wanted, and that he would be pleased if I could do anything to help while he worked on the horse. Jack went on to share the following story about me:

A woman had called me about a problem with her horse shaking it's head. After we had discussed the head shaking, I asked what was wrong with it's left hind hoof. She said, "Nothing, the horse is not lame."

I went on to tell her that the horse was telling me that her hoof was sore and felt like it had a stone bruise in it. I suggested that she might want to have the shoer take a look at it the next time he was there.

The woman called Jack and told him that she wanted him to check the horse for a stone bruise. He asked if the horse was lame. She responded "No, but some lady in Pennsylvania told me, over the phone, that the horse had a stone bruise." He managed not to laugh until he hung up the phone.

When Jack got to her farm, he picked up the left hind hoof, cleaned it out, but there was no sign of a bruise. He pulled the shoe, ran his blacksmith knife over the hoof to pare off a layer, there it was - a stone bruise, "the size of a golf ball!" That had happened several weeks earlier, he had been hoping our paths would cross so he could meet me and hear more about my work.

As Jack went back to working on the horse, I stood off to the side and tuned in on what the horse was feeling. Every so often I felt a cramp and alerted Jack so he could put the hoof down, or adjust the position of the leg. Susan had walked up to the horse, and he wanted to be near her to nuzzle and be petted. Linda got comfortable on a bench, and the rest of the shoeing job went smoothly. When the job was complete, Jack stood up in amazement, said he had never had a time with that horse that was so easy.

Jack was another horseshoer who learned quickly how to be a part of the animal. I can always remember the day I taught him. He stood for so long, with his eyes closed, after I was finished showing him a particular exercise, that I thought he did not get it. Then he opened his eyes - wide and awestruck slowly said, "Oh-my-God...." When he recovered from his overwhelming astonishment, he continued, "Now I know what to do for this horse...I was stumped...now I know." He sat quietly for a few moments, once again he got a look of total amazement. A beautiful smile spread across his face and once again he slowly stated, "Oh-my-God...." He had, indeed, traveled to the inner depth of another living being.

David Black

My friend Linda had a young horse named Socks who hated to have his hind hooves shod. She had Socks since he was a baby, and he had always been that way. When David worked on Socks he and Linda tried everything they could to keep him calm, and stop him from kicking. The only thing that worked was a twitch on his nose that was so uncomfortable that he concentrated on that instead of the shoer. Although this is not a pleasant thing to do, a shoer cannot be put in constant danger.

One day, Linda asked if I would mine being present when Socks was going to be shod. We are really good friends, so I quickly responded that I would be happy to attend. Linda told David that an animal communicator would be there to help with the hind, but he could start with the front until I arrived. He just said, "Sure," and turned away to get his tools ready.

Linda met me when I parked my truck, and told me that she was pretty sure David did not believe in animal communication, but she didn't think he would object.

Off we went to the barn, where I was introduced to David, who nodded politely. David was still gathering his equipment, so I went to have a chat with Socks. I showed him a mental picture of himself standing quietly while he was shod, and told him it would be over quickly if he cooperated. I assured him he was safe and the procedure was pain free.

Socks said he would try, but he wanted me to stand and talk to him. That was no problem. David trimmed the hoof, checked the shoe for size and went to his truck to heat the shoe in the portable furnace to hammer it into the right shape on the anvil. When he returned to the barn, Socks was standing with his hind leg dangling in the air, waiting to have the shoe put on.

David couldn't hide his amazement. He had worked on Socks many times and couldn't believe this was the same horse. The shoe needed a little more shaping, so David took it back to the truck. When he came back, the leg was once again dangling, waiting to be fitted. David was still shocked, and just as much when it happened the third time.

After Socks was done, fed treats, complimented enthusiastically, and put in his stall, David couldn't contain his enthusiasm for learning more about animal communication. He left with a handful of my cards to give to his clients.

I have a great deal of respect for horseshoers. They have to get in some rather precarious positions in doing their job. I appreciate these three gentleman and many other farriers I have met over the years.

Can I Have A Baby?

Up until I knew I was going to write a book I seldom took notes during or after a consultation. In fact the way I gathered material for the book was by requesting memories through my newsletter and as I would talk to repeat clients. There are also times when a particular consultation would make an impact on me and I was able to re-establish the story quite easily. Many times clients would write letters to me with follow-up stories, this made restructuring stories easier.

There were several reasons for this practice.

First, when someone called for a repeat call, I would not want to check to see what the problem was with the animal the last time I communicated with him or her. By the time I received the next call the first problem might be cleared up and something new happening. My mind might be centered on what I thought I was going to hear, instead of what the animal was telling me.

Second, I can't concentrate on what I'm being told and take notes at the same time. Along with that, there can be so much information coming through quickly, that it would take too long to write.

There are times when I would remember an unusual story, but I seldom connected the name of the person, the animal, and the story. One of my friends theorizes that one part of the brain interprets the messages and another part remembers - I'll bet a third part is responsible for writing.

I do keep records on clients and appointments schedules, just not specifics of those appointments. Sometimes this lack of information can manifest in interesting ways, as happened in the following chain of events:

It all began with a series of phone calls coming from either the owner or trainer of several racehorses. We would talk to each horse. The first time I talked to Geraldyne Mitchell's horse, Katie, who was a multi-winner race horse, she told me what was going on in her body. When Katie finished the rundown, she said, "Can I have a baby?"

The answer was "No" for very good reasons. Her job as a race horse was not complete, she needed to prove herself on the track. As soon as that had happened, her career would be finished and she would be ready to have a baby.

On the next call, I spoke with the trainer about a half dozen horses, and then we got to Katie. I did not remember talking to her before, but when she again asked if she could have a baby I thought to myself that another mare had asked me that one time. The trainer started to laugh, and told me that Katie had asked that the last time. The answer remained the same, Katie's racing career was not yet complete. She needed to have more patience.

More time passed, and Geraldyne called again with a list of horses. Things went along smoothly until we got to Katie. She was unhappy with the stall she had just been moved into in a new barn. She showed me a picture indicating darkness. Geraldyne explained that the group of stalls were in the center of a barn, and the new stall was darker than Katie's last stall.

Katie was told she was going to race in the next few days, and asked if she would do well. She said "No, but if I can get out in the sunshine, I will try a bit harder." Actually, she continued to explain, she didn't want to race anymore. She felt that she had run enough races, she was ready to have a baby...suddenly, I remembered our previous conversation. We chatted a bit more and I tried to encourage Katie as much as I could.

Katie ran the race, but did not do well. Geraldyne said that as Katie came down the home stretch you could see that her heart was not in the race. She also told me that there was a large sliding door not far from Katie's stall. When it was opened to let more light in the barn Katie could see a baby in the field. Geraldyne said Katie stretched and contorted her neck every way she could to keep the baby in her line of vision.

When she ran the last race poorly, it was decided that Katie's racing career was over and she was sent to a breeding farm to meet the future father of her baby.

During Geraldyne's next appointment, she shared Katie's new life. Mares and foals dotted the pastures when she arrived. You could just see how anxious she was to see the babies. I suggested we contact Katie to see how she was doing. She told me, "I'm here to pick out my baby. I told my friend Kelly (a teenager who works on the farm and is talented in the field of animal communications) that I want a light brown baby." I explained that wasn't quite how 'getting a baby' worked. Katie was disappointed, but said she understood.

I later heard that a few days after this conversation, Katie was bred and is now waiting the birth of her first foal. I know she will be a wonderful mother and will have many babies.

I Live With Toads!

I was introduced to Mary Smith at a large horse show in New Jersey. She knew about me and asked if I could talk to Sunnie for a few minutes. I agreed, and was taken to see a lovely Palomino mare who was tied in a box stall. Her head was down, and her ears were back. I couldn't understand why she was tied in her stall as this was not usual practice.

Mary requested that I ask Sunnie what was bothering her. Sunnie's stable mates were three aisles away, but Sunnie was so bad that she had to be moved to a free stall elsewhere in the facility. She had been throwing herself at the side of the stall, and trying to bite or kick the horses stabled near her.

First she had been moved to a stall on the end of the row, so no horse was behind her. This didn't work because, she had immediately thrown herself at the wall of the stall to intimidate the horse next to her. Hence, this current move where she was also tied in disgrace.

I asked her what was wrong. Sunnie responded that she was most upset because she did not even have a picture or name on this stall. "No one will know who I am."

Mary said she would bring the plaque and picture and went off to complete this task. While she was gone, Sunnie immediately brightened and showed her approval by putting her ears up.

I asked why she had attacked the horse beside her in the other stall. She said, "He is a toad. He needed to be taught a lesson, so I decided to do it."

Mary, who had returned by this time, acknowledged that the horse Sunnie was referring to had a bad habit of kicking the stall. But, Mary wondered about the horse on Sunnie's right side. Sunnie quickly answered, "He was a toad, too. I asked him something and he didn't even answer."

Mary's next question was about the horse in the stall next to Sunnie's current location. "What is wrong with this horse?"

Sunnie quickly snapped, "Talk about toads! This one is the biggest toad in the place. I really don't like her!"

At that point, Mary's husband walked up to us. Mary made the introductions, and told me that her husband usually took care of Sunnie. Then said to him, "Tell Anita what you call anyone, or anything that displeases you."

He said, "A toad!"

Sunnie's remarks reminded me of a call that I had a few years earlier. The caller had a dressage horse who knew he was beautiful and talented. He told the owner that he enjoyed doing dressage because he loved to be admired. He indicated that, "The more people who watch and appreciate me, the better I like it." The owner agreed that sounded much like the personality the horse showed.

She then asked to talk to her other horse, who was a stable mate of the first horse. This horse was quite pleasant and did not have the inflated ego of the first horse. The horse was asked what he thought of his stable mate. The immediate answer that he gave made me laugh. He said, "He's a twit."

The owner laughed and said, "Oh, that comment came from their English groom...rather accurate too, I'd say!"

The Brit

The Brit is a lovely horse who was foaled in England. He has medical problems that do not make him fit for rigorous riding, so his owner was looking for a good home for him, and a friend of mine looked at him. I was asked to consult with The Brit to ask what he thought of going to live with my friend. He thought a moment, and then said, "I will go if they want, but then I will miss the lady who wears the hat. She is coming for me shortly." No one had a clue as to who that would be, but everyone decided that The Brit would remain where he was.

Several months later a young woman, Michele Allen, who I had met several times, called for an appointment. She had an adorable, huge, mostly-Belgian horse by the name of Zeus. He used to pull a carriage in Philadelphia, but had been hit and injured by a garbage truck and could no longer continue to pull the heavy carriages. Through a long chain of events, Zeus ended up with Michele who rode him for pleasure, and even showed him occasionally in dressage classes. Zeus and Michele were soulmates and doted on each other.

When Michele called she told me that she had been given The Brit. I immediately began a conversation with the horse and asked if Michele was "the lady who wore the hat." The Brit confirmed that "Yes, in fact, she was."

I asked Michele if she was in the habit of wearing hats, and she answered, "No, not usually." However, her parents had recently moved, and her father had unearthed a goofy hat before they left. He gave it to Michele who wore it in the barn. It was nothing she would wear in public, but it kept her warm as she did her chores in the chilly mornings.

An Invisible Soda Can?

Diana Greenwell called me from Florida with a puzzling problem. Her horse would not go down the path to his paddock. He stopped at a certain point and refused to move. He had the only paddock with grass, and Diana did not want to change to one that he would go into.

I asked why he stopped, and he repeated several times, "The energy."

I asked if he could show me the energy, and I got a picture of a large cylindrical shaped object that was almost transparent, but bubbled. It almost looked like someone could stand in it and say, "Beam me up, Scotty."

I described the object to Diana, and she groaned, "Oh great, he's afraid of an invisible soda can." She thought a minute, and then asked, "All the other horses have walked through it, why won't you?"

He promptly replied, "The chestnut mare wouldn't go through that space!"

Diana had to admit the chestnut mare had acted the same way, but she had walked through the energy. The horse agreed, but said he was also scared when the mare walked through.

Later that day I was looking through my list of Flower Essence information and I saw a remedy listed for animals who showed these tendencies. I called Diana and told her about it, and suggested that she might want to look into this possible solution herself. She agreed, and also added that she had been doing some research and had found out some interesting information. She believed the horse next door had died earlier. She said that horse's paddock gate was open, the horse was gone, and there was a back hoe in the field.

Was that the energy her horse felt?

The Bleachers

Winston was a talented bay Thoroughbred gelding who could jump in beautiful form. However, Winston had a problem. Sometimes he would behave beautifully in the show ring, and other times he became totally out of control. Carol DiGuiseppe called me as a last resort to try to figure out what set Winston off. She felt that if she knew the circumstances she could figure out what to do to correct the problem.

Winston told me he did not like the bleachers behind the glass because they reminded him of the race track. He continued, "In fact I don't like the track at all and do not want to race."

I found out in a later conversation that Carol had recently moved to a barn that had Plexiglas half way around the ring, and there were bleachers behind it. That was one of the places that Winston acted terrible. He was also very difficult to handle at a show that had a "stadium effect" with bleachers all around.

I also told Carol that Winston was belligerent. She agreed!

Carol decided to delve into Winston's racing background. We talked after her investigation and she had some interesting tidbits of information.

Winston had trained at a track in New York, but it was obvious that he did not like race training. He did so poorly in training, and was so belligerent, that he never did get to race.

The way from the stable area to the track was through a tunnel. The first thing you saw as you emerged from the tunnel was bleachers. Carol knew that when a horse is afraid at that point it is not a good sign that he will go on to be a race horse.

Carol and I had discussed the fact that there is no picture for the word "don't." I suggested that "don't" might have played a big part in his early training. I explained that this thought picture needed to be re-communicated in a positive manner to help overcome Winston's fear.

I continued with this explanation: Someone had called me about a dog that ran in the street. I asked the dog why he did that, and he said, "She tells me to."

I asked the owner what she said to the dog, and she said, "Don't run in the street." I suggested that she tell the dog to stay on the sidewalk, which was a clear picture of what she wanted. The next day she called to tell me that it worked! The dog kept looking back at her as if he was waiting for the command to run into the street, but it did not come, and the dog did not run out.

When Carol and I spoke later, she told me that Winston had made radical progress in his behavior. When Carol was training him she used all positive phrases. After he went over a few jumps she congratulated him on a job well done. She told him that the people in the bleachers came out to admire his beauty, and watch him jump.

Winston started acting like a new horse, and it was noticed during the show season by other riders. Nobody, other than Carol, had expected Winston to behave over the jump courses, and now he was winning consistently. Winston's improvement, although still in progress, has been appreciated by judges and competitors.

Mystery Of The Hives

I had met a very talented young woman who rode a horse who was also quite talented. We talked about animal communication, and she was interested in the subject. Several months later she called me about her horse.

She had been competing the horse in Europe and, after one of the events, noticed that the horse's lower leg was bleeding. It was not a big problem, and was taken care of quickly. The next day the horse had hives everywhere except where his blanket covered him. The following day the hives were worse, and even more so the day after that.

The horse's handler believed it was some kind of allergic reaction. The first day the horse had his feed changed, the next day his bedding was changed. There were changes in the water, water bucket, feed bucket, stall, and barn, but the hives persisted.

When the horse was brought home to the States he was routinely gone over by a veterinarian, who could not help but see the hives. He suggested that the feed should be changed.

The young woman was terribly upset as she was due to try out for the Olympics and knew it would be about thirty days of trying changes before the horse could be treated. It had been decided that the horse was having an allergic reaction, but none of the changes did any good, so it was not environmental.

I was called in to consult at this point. I asked the horse if he could tell me anything, and he said, "I have white dashes in my blood."

I promised the young woman I would do what I could to help the horse. The first thing I did was to track down one of the veterinarians that I knew who looked after this horse and believed in animal communications.

The veterinarian asked the horse a series of questions about the white dashes. When the horse was asked the first question as to whether it was a certain bacteria, he said "No." The second question was also "No." The third question, he said "Yes, that's what the dashes are."

The veterinarian then asked how the horse felt when he received a treatment the previous day, and the horse said, "It felt like the top of my head was going to be blown off."

The veterinarian explained that was because of the way the medication was given, and what was in it. The veterinarian asked the horse, "How much good did the treatment do?"

The horse replied that one third of the white dashes were destroyed. The veterinarian responded with, "That's perfect. This is a three dose treatment, and only one dose was given, can you get through two more treatments?" The horse indicated that if that was necessary to cure this problem, he would certainly cooperate.

The hives were quickly cleared up and the horse returned to compete successfully.

Other Animals

Lovie

Lynn had a rabbit rescue operation. Lovie was one of her favorite rabbits. Lovie had been quite ill for several weeks when Lynn called to ask if I could intervene by asking her some questions.

Lynn wanted to know if Lovie felt she would pull through, and if there was anything else Lynn could do to help. Lovie responded, "Yes, I'm going to recover, but I feel I need a vitamin to help with that recovery." She then showed me a brownish liquid in a dropper bottle. This, she said would "do the trick."

Lynn understood immediately since this confirmed what she had been thinking. They were both referring to alfalfa. Lovie also expressed a desire to eat bread. Lynn said she did not give bread to her, but Lovie still insisted that she wanted bread.

Lynn also wondered about Lovie's age. She had been given the rabbit by someone who had found her abandoned and wandering around a parking lot. Lovie was happy to respond that she was four years old and had plenty of time left.

A few days later, Lynn called to say that it was pretzels that Lovie liked, and the ingredients would be similar to bread. Lovie had eagerly eaten the pretzels that were offered. The combination seemed to be "just what the rabbit ordered" and Lovie was soon feeling back to herself.

Freddie

For a while, I worked at an Arabian breeding farm that my friend Jean Grim managed. I had just retired, wasn't willing to give up the routine of daily work, and Jean was short-handed.

When I first started to work there I wanted to fill the water buckets in the morning while the horses were out in the pasture. I was told not to in the spring because mealy worms always showed up in the buckets. Sometimes there would be six or seven in one bucket. The horses made faces when the water got low, and let us know they did not like the worms in there.

Although most of the stories I have shared with you in this book have been about domestic animals, I don't limit my conversations only to them. When I go for a walk, or sometimes even driving in my car, I'll chat with any animal who is willing to enter into conversation. I might be shy with people, but not at all when it comes to animals.

Jean also communicates with animals and we had already had several conversations with one of the resident sparrows that nested in the beams above the stalls. This sparrow had told us earlier that he was formally Jean's dog, Freddie, who had chosen to come back as a bird. He had not liked the restrictions that went along with being a dog, and felt that he would be happier and freer as a bird.

Since there were many sparrows living in the rafters, I asked Freddie how we could tell which one he was. He said he would fly in by the paddock door on the second stall, and then give us a sign.

An hour later Jean was body clipping a very young filly. In order to have the filly stand quietly, Jean sang to her with her lovely soothing voice. As I held the filly's lead shank and listened to Jean sing, I looked up and saw a sparrow fly in the door Freddie had told us about. He flew to the top of the stall closest to us and began to sing with Jean.

Now that Freddie had identified himself, I asked him what he might know about the mealy worms. He said the birds dipped them into the buckets of water to provide moisture when they ate the worms. He told us that they could not judge the depth of the water, and sometimes dropped them and could not get them back.

We discussed the problem this was causing and then I asked if the birds could dip them in the shallow bowls of water on the floor. He thought it was pretty funny that I would ask birds to stand over the cats bowls and concentrate on making their food better. Didn't I know cats ate birds?

I had to admit that I had not come up with the smartest solution. Freddie came up with a better one. There were other places on the property where there was shallow water, and he would tell the birds to dip the worms there. After that Jean and I rarely ever found a mealy worm in the water buckets. When we would, we just figured it was due to a newcomer.

Insect Problems Solved

Working at the Arabian farm gave me ample opportunity to communicate with many animals, but the gnats were really different! I was cleaning a section outside of the barn where the horses stood frequently. As I was clearing the manure away I was besieged with gnats. They were trying to get in my ears, up my nose, and I didn't dare open my mouth. This was really frustrating, and I was trying to figure out how to resolve the problem.

Then I remembered being at one of Penelope Smith's workshops when she talked about the collective consciousness of insects. I had nothing to lose by talking to the gnats, so I asked to communicate with, "...the one who is in charge of all the gnats in this area." I did not know whether I would be in touch with a male or female, and did not want to offend anyone. After all, I was going to ask for a favor.

I did not see a particular gnat or image a particular insect, but I diligently continued to explain that I had a job to do. I would do it as quickly as possible and then leave. Could they please leave me alone until I was finished. Suddenly I was gnatless - and quite surprised.

Several days later Jean and I were walking through a pasture and we became the focus of a large swarm of gnats. I told Jean not to worry, I knew what to do. I explained what to say, and we both recited the request for immunity. In a flash, all the gnats left me and swarmed around Jean's head. I knew she was not pleased, but I couldn't help laughing.

Personal Hygiene

Dorinda called from Baton Rouge, Louisiana for an appointment regarding her parrots. Dorinda asked her African Grey, Samantha, whether she liked to be sprayed or immersed in water to bathe. It was a trick question. Dorinda knew Samantha did not like to be sprayed, and would not get her in water.

The answer, however, came as a surprise. Samantha said that she did not like the spray, and did not like the color of the bowl Dorinda offered her for bathing. I asked what color she wanted, and I was shown a light color that I thought might be a pale yellow. I told Dorinda, and she said she was willing to buy Samantha a yellow bowl if that would help.

Dorinda wrote to me and said: "Remember the discussion with Samantha regarding her bathing? I finally figured out what she wanted was the bowl she bathed in when she was a baby. It was a white Corningware bowl - not big enough for her now but - if she likes it, so what! Once I put it out she hopped right in. I couldn't believe it. She had not even put a toe in the water for at least a year, maybe longer. It was very gratifying to see her play in the water."

Traveling Conversations

With my guest appearances, I get to travel frequently. When I am on the road, I enjoy visiting animal gathering sites (zoos, aquariums and the like). On one such trip, I took the opportunity to visit the Baltimore Aquarium and watched the dolphin show. I wondered what they had to say about their environment. I was pleased to find they were content with their living arrangement and enjoyed their work.

It was difficult to get any communication during the show, but one thing I did pick up clearly made me laugh. One of the dolphins had done his part of the act well, and was rewarded with some fish. The second dolphin then did his trick and received his fish reward. As the second dolphin was receiving his prize I could hear the first dolphin counting the fish.

Can dolphins actually count? I don't know. I believe I interpret the information I get from the animals into my own concept and language. I am sure that the dolphin knew, in his own form of intelligence, how many fish he had received, and how many his friend had been awarded. He was making sure his friend did not get more than he had.

Even though I interpret and explain to people what I believe the animal has told me, there have been times that I have used a word and have been corrected by the animal. Once I said, "He believes..." and was corrected, *"Tell her I know!"* This tells me that I am allowed to explain the best I can, but if I get it wrong I will have to make it right!

Eat your greens

Erika had an iguana, Fluffy, who had stopped eating. When I made mental contact with him my body felt sluggish and I did not want to move. When I asked why he was not eating, Fluffy told me he wanted green vegetables that did not taste so bitter. I showed him an image of Swiss chard, and he said he would like that. He also wanted more room as he was feeling too crowded in his tank.

Erika put some Swiss chard in his tank and he ate it at once. She also made other arrangements that gave him more space, and he became happy again. Sometimes the little things in life can make all the difference, not only to humans, but to our animal companions as well.

Maturing Guinea Pigs

Angel and Crystal lived with Kelly Duffy from the time they were about six weeks old. Their cage door was left open so they could explore their environment and come and go at will.

Crystal was at first calmer than Angel. She was quieter and less prone to squeal for no clear reason. Angel has always been intense. She would squeal very loudly if she thought she was going to be picked up, or for no particular reason. She had a good appetite for alfalfa pellets and raw vegetables, but when she was out of her cage she had been chewing on everything - molding, carpeting, and furniture.

Angel had begun to calm down for a couple of weeks, not jumping at her own shadow, and was somewhat less vocal and less apprehensive about being near humans. Then she began freaking out over everything. She also frantically began to look for a way to get under the living room sofa, something that had not interested her previously. When she would get under there, she would not come out. The more Kelly tried to prevent Angel from going under the sofa, the more she wanted to go.

Crystal had always been less intense. She was not nearly as jumpy or frightened of her own shadow as Angel. She was also much less apprehensive about being picked up than Angel. Shortly after Angel began showing this strange behavior, Crystal began exhibiting the same behavior. In addition to the crawling under the couch, their nervousness increased about being picked up. They nervously began chewing electric appliance cords, houseplants, and anything they could get their teeth on. They were also starting to run and hide in other parts of the apartment to get away from their people.

Kelly considered sending them to a new home, but thought she would try animal communications first. As soon as I made contact with the two Guinea pigs I was aware that they were experiencing their first menstrual cycles. Angel was almost through, and Crystal was in the middle of hers. I suggested Kelly might want to consult some holistic modalities, such as Flower Essences, for a possible calming solution.

Kelly reported later that she had found a remedy and made up the mixture and put it in a spray bottle. She sprayed their cage and food. Within a day both pigs became much more settled. They stopped trying to get under the sofa, and Angel became much less verbally agitated. They did continue to chew things, but their behavior was no longer as out of control as it had been.

Kelly noted that in the future she could now be more in tune to the Guinea pigs mood swings and act accordingly.

Lost & Found

I personally debated long and hard as to including this chapter in the book. Some communicators enjoy trying to locate missing animals, but at times I find myself feeling the pain of the person who has called me. It is difficult for me to release the anxiety that comes over me when I do one of these communications because I want so much to reunite the person and the missing companion. The other part of the personal anxiety is that I seldom hear the outcome as to confirmation regarding whether the animal is found, so I am left with the wondering. It is far easier for me to take the kind of call where I tell the person where the animal feels pain, or what it wants to say, and get immediate feedback.

This is not usually how things happen with lost or missing pets. The person always wants to know if the animal is dead or alive. Sometimes the pet does not know. This is especially true if it has died quickly, as in an accident, so that makes the call that much harder. The next question is often, "Is he close to home, or far away?" Animal communications does not seem to have the same sense of time and space as we are used to in everyday life, so this is also a hard question to answer.

Sometimes I get a follow-up call, such as, "The cat said he would be home before morning, and sure enough, he showed up," but other times I don't get a call. I have dowsed maps and pinpointed areas and later learned that the animal was sighted in that area.

Then there are times when I make a connection with the animal and learn that it wishes to remain away and not return to the people companions with whom he had been residing. The animal generally has very good reasons, but this is very difficult to relay to grieving people.

However, missing pets are an important part of animal communication, and I will put my feelings aside and tell of some of the interesting ones I have encountered.

The Funeral - With A Happy Ending

One of my local clients called while a thunderstorm was heading toward her town. Her neighbor had gone on a trip and left her three dogs with someone else in the neighborhood. My client feared the dog sitter was not responsible enough for the job. Sure enough, one of the dogs became upset by the storm, slipped out of the yard, and was gone. My client asked if I could contact the Sheltie, and ask where she was. I sensed a large building with white siding. It was not a house, but too big for a garage or shed.

The client said she knew where it was. It had to be the storage building behind the local high school. She would go there immediately. She called back in an hour and said she did not see the dog. By that time the storm was over my house and I was not willing to stay on the phone. I told her I would call her back when it passed, but she said "No" she would go back out in the morning to search again.

My phone rang late the next morning. The client said, "We found the dog. She was in the cemetery across the street from the storage building. She was attending a Lutheran funeral."

With heartfelt joy and laughter, I told the client how happy I was that they had located the dog, and speculated as to whether the dog might have known the deceased. The prompt reply was, "Oh, no. The dog is Catholic!"

The Unfortunate Jack Russell Terrier

A woman called about a missing Jack Russell. From the outset, I did not have a good feeling about this one. I could sense there was a steep bank of a stream and a tree with exposed roots. I could not see any of it in my mind, but knew it was there. I described the scene to the caller, and she said there was a fallen tree near a steep bank, and the roots were sticking out. Her other dogs had been animated when they were near that tree the day before, but not on the day she called me.

I suggested that she go back and dig again near where the branches stuck out from the tree. When she called back she told me she and her husband found a hole and dug it out until they could see the body of the little dog. She had smothered in the hole.

Although it is always difficult to find the animal that has died, I believe it is worse not to know. I offered my condolences and thanked the lady for letting me know the outcome.

Delaware Dog

A newspaper in Delaware carried a story about another Jack Russell Terrier who had been washed, or jumped overboard from a boat. My number was given to the grieving person, and she contacted me.

I felt the dog had bounced off when the water was choppy, and swam for the shore. There were branches from a submerged tree that snagged his collar and he drowned. I asked if she had been any place where this could happen. I could picture a point of land where trees grew almost to the water. She said they had been in the river, so it could have been any one of several places.

At my request, the woman made a list of areas along the route they had sailed, and called me back. I was prepared with my tools for dowsing the places she would identify as specifically where they had been boating.

As the woman read the list slowly, the sinker remained still. She gave me one name, and it suddenly started to swing fast. When I told her that this was the place the dog went overboard, she said the place fit my description perfectly. Although I never heard the outcome, from the information I had communicated, and the lady's confirmation of the site, I doubt if they were ever able to locate his body.

The dog did tell me that he wanted to be reincarnated. I later learned that his mother was bred and became pregnant the day he died.

Tiny Cats

One day I received a call from a woman who shared her home with a large number of animal companions. The household consisted of nine cats and several dogs. The woman assured me that it was a happy environment and both humans and animals got along very well together. It was a home filled with love and respect for each individual.

This is why the situation was very unusual. Two of the cats were now missing for three weeks. It was not usual for any of the family to be away for more than a day or two, but no one was ever gone more than a few days at a time. The two cats in question, however, were runts in their litter and had remained very small. They both spent most of their time together and always remained close to home.

I was quickly able to contact both cats, who were still together. I asked them to tell me what they could, and they said they were "lifted." I could not see a hand, or clothing of whoever might have lifted them. This was puzzling, so I asked the caller if she had any owls in the area. She responded that "Yes" they did. Even though I could not hear the sound of wings, I still felt an owl, or a large hawk had lifted each of them, and killed quickly from behind.

The caller said that made sense, since another cat, who was a little larger, had come home recently with a strange scrape on the top of her head. There were owls and hawks in the area, and she speculated that the owl had tried to pick this cat up too and she had gotten away.

The caller asked if the cats remained together and if they were happy. Both cats responded with affirmative answers and said to please tell their family that they sent their love and that they would keep a watch over them from their new home.

The Old Dog

When an animal has disappeared, the voices of those calling usually carry a tone of despair, but the voice on the other end of the line on this chilly November night was frantic. The little dog who had wandered off hours ago was old, deaf, and nearly blind.

The call was from another state, so I asked the caller if they had rain recently as I had a sensation of slimy mud on my hands that seeped up between my fingers. The picture in my mind looked like a gully.

The caller said there had been no rain but the ground in the nearby woods was usually wet, and there was a stream that ran through the woods. I suggested that she look there for the dog.

Within a half hour my phone rang. The caller's voice was now joyous instead of frantic. She found the dog standing by the stream, safe and ready to go home.

1962, Target, my first horse, and I go over a jump bareback

My first ride on Suzie - November 1944

Porcia

Jean Grim welcomes Elfie into the world

Ron and Linda Briel treating a horse

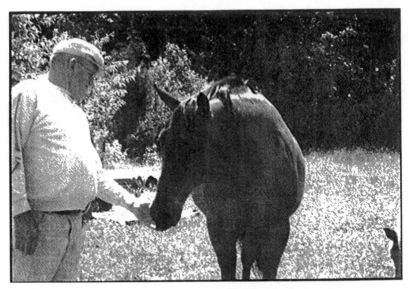

My husband Vic and Colonel share a moment

*Our son Joe and
Puppy 1985*

Joe and The Madam

Brady Benninghoff

Huit inspects a cleaning job

Tara

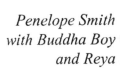

*Penelope Smith
with Buddha Boy
and Reya*

BB and her "best friend" Fancy

Judith Shoemaker, D.V.M. working with an Airedale

*Jean Grim's
horse Sands*

Porcia, doing "horse stuff"

*Tigger
Ajamian*

Cassie Ajamian

Vic and Seven 1991

Smokey the first horse to send me messages

Dopey peeks out of the barn "with the red in it"

BB, age 2, investigates a noise

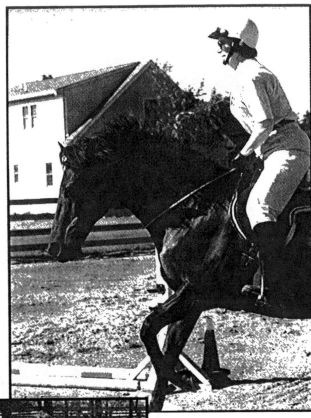

Susan Rifkin
Ajamian
riding Richie
without a
bridle

Donna Lozito and
Sweet Dreams spending
time together

The Vet Connection

I have always been hesitant about telling veterinarians about my animal communications work. I have felt that most of them have been trained not to believe it exists. However, once, during a late evening visit, when no one else was in the waiting room, I told the young woman veterinarian about my work. She seemed receptive, so I gave her my card.

She left that practice shortly after that meeting. Sometime later, after one of my lectures, one of the attendees came up to me and asked if I remembered this veterinarian. I affirmed that I did. The individual stated that the veterinarian had planned to attend the lecture, but other obligations had gotten in the way. She sent her fond regards.

Another few years passed and I received a phone call from the same veterinarian. She had just moved to a new home and her inside cat was missing. He had been gone for over a week, and was possibly sighted once. The cat that was seen was the same color, but far away.

I told her that a black dog had chased the cat, and she said it was her dog. She would be glad to put the dog in the house so the cat would come back into the yard. She was going to do that as soon as we hung up.

I got the picture of a plowed field. The time of year was late fall, and she said there was a field with winter wheat growing in it. I told her that the field I saw was soil that was turned over, with no crop planted. There were woods behind the field and I was certain the cat was in those woods.

She knew where that field was, and it was not the direction that they had been going to hunt for the cat. They would take flashlights and go out immediately. I said I would ask the cat to go home.

The phone rang a half hour later. The veterinarian said the cat, "Had his face buried in a dish of cat food." He was coming from the woods, across the plowed field when they found him.

For some reason, my connection with this veterinarian continues. May it always be with a happy ending.

Lucky Dog

One bitter cold winter day I got a call about a missing German Shepherd. She was an old dog, and had been gone for two days. There were a couple of busy highways in the neighborhood, and the owner was in a state of panic.

I felt the dog was alive, but all I could see was brick buildings. The owner said her home was located on several acres of ground, but there were shopping centers nearby that had brick stores. She had searched there, but to no avail. She went back home and called the police and animal shelters once more.

The next day she called to tell me that the dog had been found near a brick apartment building, just sitting under a tree and waiting. Everyone who saw her thought she belonged to someone else in the building, so no one tried to help her. Finally, someone realized that she had been sitting in the same place too long, and called the police. The police had no trouble identifying the dog from the owners information. This made the reunion very easy. The grateful person and animal companion were quickly and happily reunited.

Stories I've Been Told

People often refer to my animal communication skills as my gift. Perhaps it is a gift, but it is a gift that we all have within us. I have studied hard and practiced long to develop my abilities. Two way telepathic communicating was something I learned to do - and something I now teach to others..

I believe that Early Man did not have vocal cords developed enough to be able to communicate much through speech; therefore, he must have used mental telepathy. The *wiring* of our mind must still include the ability to use telepathy, so we have to be able to reach into an old trunk somewhere in the dusty attic of our brain and reactivate those wires. Once we get them cleaned up, and practice using them again, they start to fully operate.

Our minds are capable of doing so much more than we are aware of, and animal communications has led to expanding many other facets in my life. When I find something new to learn it seems as if a door to another dimension opens just wide enough for me to peek through and see wondrous new sights. As I become more adept, the door swings open and I can enter that dimension. My life becomes fuller each day!

I am grateful to Penelope Smith for her insights and wisdom, and her generosity in sharing her talent with the rest of the world. What I teach is the Basic Workshop that Penelope created, and add some other information that I have picked up in my travels through this life.

I have also developed an advanced workshop, but it is still based on Penelope's basic principles. The one thing that does not change is my love of watching people light up with joy as they realize that they can have telepathic communications with an animal.

I encourage everyone to communicate with animals. When I started to write this book I put a note in my newsletter asking readers who had been clients to refresh my memory on consultations we had since I don't make it a habit of taking notes during communications. Also anyone who had interesting experiences of their own were requested to get in touch.

I was delighted to hear from so many people with stories of what happened with their own communications experiences. I've selected a number of these stories to encourage you to explore your personal abilities to communicate with your animal companions. They are waiting for this

Remember the principles, meditate to become centered, always ask permission of the animal, and then be open to the *visual* communication you will receive. It might not always be the typical responses we are expecting when we verbally communicate as people, but if you are open you will soon recognize what is being relayed.

Ready For A New Dog

My client, Shirley Rodgers had recently lost her dog companion. She had done her healing from the loss and woke up one morning with the feeling this was the day she was ready to get another dog. She called me and I confirmed that her dog was looking for her. Shirley went out and picked up a friend who said, "You need to get a dog today."

When Shirley got home from doing her errands she called some local shelters looking for the type of dog she wanted. She then went to her local SPCA and asked for an older dog. They brought Angel out and Shirley said, "Angel looked at me as if to say, 'What took you so long?'" Angel looked at the door and back to Shirley. When they got in the car Angel settled down as if she had been with Shirley all of her life.

The Horse Trial

Terry Pisano told me a story about a horse she rode in a horse trial. Her nephew who was also at the event, stated that had he not witnessed the horse's actions he would have never believed it. I agreed that it is a pretty amazing tale.

In preparation for the event, Terry had walked the course on foot twice so that she would remember the sequence of the jumps she had to take. Some of the jumps were side by side, but different heights for multiple levels of competition, so she also had to remember which side of the jump to go over.

While Terry was grooming her horse and getting ready for the trial she recited the course to herself out loud to review and further plant the memory in her brain. However, when she was riding the course, and got to the fifth fence, she saw one of the judges standing by a fence other than the one she thought she should be taking. Terry quickly decided that she had been wrong about her memory of the course, and headed for the wrong fence.

The horse made a 180 degree turn, against her signal to him, pulled his head so that she lost hold of the reins, and steered himself over the rest of the course, taking the correct fences.

They placed fourth, but would have been eliminated from the competition if they had gone the way Terry wanted!

Sonny's Peaches

Linda Briel has been to several of my workshops, and is also a close friend. Linda has a *guest horse* (a horse that can be ridden when a friend comes to ride with you), Sonny, whom I ride once in a while. One day I went to Linda's to ride with her. Halfway there I realized that I had forgotten to bring carrots for Sonny. I was driving right by a produce stand, so I pulled in and asked for carrots. Not only were there no carrots, there was not even an apple in the place. I bought some peaches, and went on my way.

When Linda and I were in the barn I offered Sonny a peach while I told Linda the carrot story. She started to say that horses don't eat peaches, but was stopped by Sonny whisking the peach out of my outstretched hand. He closed his eyes with pleasure and chewed slowly, peach juice pouring from his now sticky lips. Sonny was in heaven. After our ride the remaining peaches were split between the two horses who ate them eagerly.

The next day Linda was working on her fence, fixing a problem with a post. Her work was not difficult, and she had sort of blanked out most thoughts. In her mind she heard a loud, deep voice say, "Peach!" Linda looked up and was eye-to-eye with Sonny, as he put his face next to hers.

Linda raced for her kitchen to get a peach, and Sonny waited until she got back with it. After he ate his treat he contentedly wandered off to nibble grass again.

Sox Has Some Fun

Linda's husband, Ron, also had some communication experiences with his horse, Sox. Ron noticed that Sox was standing by the watering trough one day. Ron was cleaning stalls, and noticed when he wheeled the barrow out, a few minutes later, that Sox had not moved. He received the thought from Sox, "Come see me."

Ron was pleased, so he walked right over to pet Sox. As soon as Ron reached him, Sox opened his mouth and slobbered water all over Ron. He had been standing for at least five minutes with the water in his mouth, waiting to get Ron to come near him.

His mouth empty, Sox said, "I was funny, wasn't I?"

Squirrels In The Attic

Janice Smith, of Washington, D.C. is about the only person I am aware of who took my communications workshop, but did not have an animal companion. Although she loved animals, she was not able to have one at that time.

Janice might not have had a pet, but she did have a problem with squirrels in the attic of her home. She had resorted to spraying an ammonia solution to repel the squirrels, and discourage them from trying to get in. She also put wire mesh over the areas where they entered.

A year after the spraying Janice heard the sound of chewing on the wire mesh. She looked and saw a squirrel. Janice made eye contact with the critter and visualized ammonia being sprayed and the squirrel running away.

Janice turned away...the squirrel left - never to return.

Irish

Mimi Gerrard was kind enough to send the following letter about her horse Irish:

"Last spring, Irish and I were looking forward to a wonderful summer and dressage show season. After four years of trying to show him as a hunter, I had finally figured out that he really didn't like jumping. (...I was slow to hear what he was trying to tell me.) Our dressage training was coming along great and Irish was happy. At our first dressage show, he seemed to strut arrogantly as if to say, 'I know I'm beautiful.' It was as if we had found a calling.

"Then with no warning, everything fell apart. Irish became evasive and rude whenever we began to work. Worst of all he was flicking his head constantly and would even try to strike his face with his front legs in the middle of a canter stride. My trainer and I were at a loss trying to figure out what the problem was. We tried everything...fly masks... riding indoors...a visit to an equine chiropractor/veterinarian.

"When nothing seemed to work, I called Anita. I asked her to ask Irish what the problem was. Immediately, she said, "Is Irish having allergy problems?" I'm always surprised at how quickly Anita can zoom in on the problem. I said 'Yes, but...what he was allergic to?' 'He says it's the dust. He has sinus problems and headaches,' Anita responded quickly. 'Does he have a window in his stall?' 'He does.' 'I can see the dust particles in the sunlight from the window.'

"The problem could have easily been solved at that point...but I decided to take Irish to a large equine medical facility in New Jersey to *really* find out what he was allergic to. Hundreds of dollars later and over fifty needle pricks in his shaved neck, the allergy tests showed that Irish was extremely allergic to - you guessed it - dust. It's hard to remain skeptical about communicating with animals when the problem is validated scientifically.

"...Irish [has been moved] to a smaller, private barn where he can spend most of his day turned out, the owners are fanatics about minimizing the dust inside. His allergies have disappeared, we are back on track with our training and looking forward to the upcoming show season.

"Thanks Anita."

Which Horse To Buy...

The following is from a letter from Elise O'Shea, who is learning from her horse through yet another means of communication. Elise was shopping for a new mount and had looked at two Fjord horses. (A Fjord horse, originally from Western Norway, is a tireless worker on farms. They are used in harness, often ridden and also used as pack animals.)

"I had [the choice of] two horses, Hush and Mehar. Mehar was eleven and had done it all. Hush was six...had good experience, but had not seen it all yet. Mehar was the type of horse my trainer/teacher wanted me to get....

"When we talked to Mehar he couldn't understand the concept of *one owner* because he had been bounced back and forth from many already. He was a good and honest soul. Mostly he wanted to trail ride. "When I saw Mehar he was very overweight...[but] when I rode him I was relaxed...and confident.

"When I saw Hush it was different. There was a connection and even though he made me nervous, I really liked him. His energy was at a higher level spiritually than Mehar, and I was looking for a match on many levels. I was buying one horse...for [a] life time.

"I was in a quandary because common sense and logic said buy Mehar. I... talked to Hush's owners many times...he had almost been sold, but they refused the sale because it didn't 'feel right.' It seemed as if Hush had been waiting for me, but Mehar was the only logical choice....

"When we talked to Hush he was a perfect gentleman. He was very intelligent and had a good vocabulary. He had a cosmic message for me about learning a new way to be in my relationships...it was his mission to give me this message. As far as buying him...[he] said it was not necessary that I buy him. It was up to me. 'Yes, I would like to come but it is not too imperative.'

"I loved the way this horse talked...

"The lesson he spoke to me about was 'balance.' I was at a crossroad in my marriage and under great pressure - to NOT be pressured was a balm to me.

"Hush said he knew me from 'a long time ago'." Here are some notes from his message:

"Our connection had to be made so I could give you this message: 'You have an insecurity. This can be surmounted and that lesson will help you with something else you must do. It has to do with balance. *Practice* will bring an end to this insecurity.'

"I have been working on his message ever since on many levels. He also told me I was comfortable as a rider....

"Hush has felt like a special gift to me...I feel *hushed* after working with him...the relationship between Hush and I often models the way I am dealing with my life. He is a great compass and healer for me.

"[Yes]...I bought Hush. I'm catching up to him with my skills. I called the woman who is selling Mehar...[s]he decided to make him fit and only sell him to someone who wanted to primarily trail ride and who would hopefully not sell him again, so Mehar benefit[ed] as well."

Tattletale

Georgianna Spayd attended one of my communications workshops. She had walked in knowing she wouldn't be able to communicate. Well, that is not how the story turned out.

Contrary to what she knew, she did quite well at the workshop. In fact she was anxious to get home to try her new skills on her cat companions.

Shortly thereafter, Georgianna called to ask, "How do you turn it off?!" What a great story...

"Although I'm still a beginner at communicating with animals, I have had a number of interesting experiences...[this one was particularly fun].

"One day before I left home I scolded my three cats about jumping up on the kitchen counter and table. Hopping into my truck, I didn't give it another thought.

"As I drove down the road my cat, Zack, suddenly popped into my head and made his presence known. I told him I wanted to concentrate on my driving...he would have to wait. He insisted...so I asked him what he wanted.

"He said my kitten, Silvester, was on the kitchen table and he didn't want to be blamed for it. I reassured him that he wouldn't be blamed, and that I would be home soon.

"Being told that an animal can talk to a person and sometimes cannot be ignored, and experiencing it are two different things. After this event I look forward to many more in the future. Talking with my animals has become a valuable part of my life with them."

Animals Helping Others

I stood by the window one winter day and watched our old gelding show the yearling filly how to dig into the snow to find the grass that was buried beneath it. She watched him paw and dig, and then she tried it. They spent several hours, side by side, finding cold green grass to eat. There were laps of hay in their stalls, but this was a new experience for the filly, and she learned quickly from the old horse.

I had read many accounts of animals helping each other, and I knew that animals taught others, but I have learned more about how they care for *all* their companions.

My son received a kitten as a gift for his twenty-first birthday. We had gone to the numbering system for cat names, and asked the kitten if it was okay to name him "Seven." He said it was fine, so everyone, except for my husband, called him that. My husband calls all cats "Libby," which became confusing when we were later adopted by a second cat.

Seven was a fun loving kitten, and fit right into the family. When asked, he said his purpose was to help our dog in her final months of life, as she was in failing health. He took his job seriously, and alerted us several times when Puppy, our old dog, was not well. Seven was always respectful of Puppy, and helped her without making physical contact. Puppy had a loving and gentle passing, and Seven has continued to be a caring cat companion to my son.

I had communicated with other animals who looked after each other, but the animals who helped a Jack Russell terrier named Frolic were amazing.

Frolic's person is a veterinarian, Judith Shoemaker. Judith had given Frolic a home after his original owner died, and no one else wanted the feisty snappy little dog, who was almost thirteen years old. A little over two years later, when Frolic was fifteen, he started to have health problems.

Judith doctored Frolic, and kept him as well as possible, but he developed a cough that kept getting worse over a period of about four months. Judith had to spend several days away from home lecturing and teaching. She called me to ask Frolic if he was going to live until she returned. He responded, "Yes, but not much longer than that."

I promised to check in with him while Judith was away and let his sitter know if anything was wrong. Each day I felt the pain in his chest, but he assured me that he would be there when Judith came back, and he was.

Weeks later it was evident that Frolic was failing rapidly. He coughed so much that he got little sleep, and he had started to have seizures. Judith was too close to the case to feel sure that she was giving him the proper medication, so she called to ask Porcia (a horse friend whose story can be found in Part II) for feedback. Judith was ordering some homeopathic remedies and wanted to know if Porcia had any other ideas.

Porcia listened to the list of remedies that Judith had considered, and either said "Yes" or "No" as she heard the name. I noticed that Judith usually said the yes ones had already been her choice. On one occasion Porcia said the medication was a good choice, but to wait three days before using it.

Judith had just started using one new medication. Porcia suggested Judith use it as steam. Judith said she would do this. When Judith asked if there was anything else she could do, Porcia showed me a mental image of a green velvet bag with medicine in it. Judith said that one of the remedies came in a green velvet box, and it was being administered.

Porcia said the only other thing was "a honey colored liquid." Judith did not know what she meant, but Porcia said she would learn.

In the meantime Judith's cat, William FitzBengal, was helping at home. Each day he would approach Frolic and stretch his legs until he had a paw on Frolic's chest or abdomen. He did not knead or put his claws out, he simply held his paws on Frolic for twenty minutes in a position much like someone sending the healing energy of Reiki, or one of the other alternative modalities. One time when Frolic was on a pillow, William had to really stretch to reach him, and his head was bent in an awkward position, but he held on for the twenty minutes.

Frolic wanted to hang on to life, and was eating heartily, so Porcia agreed that Judith should keep on helping him rather than euthanize him. A few days after our first conversation, Judith heard about an appropriate medication that was *a honey colored liquid,* she ordered it at once. This happened on a weekend. The remedies were to be delivered Tuesday morning.

I was awakened Monday at four a.m. with a backache. I tossed and turned, trying to find a position that did not hurt. I finally became awake enough to rationalize that I had no reason to be in pain since I do not have back problems. As I tried to figure out what was going on, I saw Frolic's face in my mind. I knew he was sending for me. He told me he had enough and did not want to live any longer. He wanted Judith to help him leave. I promised that I would tell her. I looked at the clock. It was now 4:30 a. m., too early to call her.

When I called Judith later in the morning she told me that Frolic had the worst seizures ever between four and four-thirty that morning. She believed that he was ready to leave because he had stopped eating. Frolic had been better during the days than nights, and this day was no different.

The homeopathic remedies were not due to be delivered until the next morning, so Judith decided to leave Frolic be and see how he managed during the night. She would be ready to help him make the transition if he needed that, but she hoped he could hold out one more night.

He couldn't. Judith called me about eight that night, and I asked Frolic what he wanted to do. He was weak and tired, but he wanted Judith to know that he would be back soon as a very fat female Jack Russell puppy. This time they would have many years to spend together.

Frolic and Judith said their good-byes, and then Judith helped him out of his pain.

The medicine that was supposed to arrive the next morning, didn't...she knew she had made the correct decision.

I just heard from Judith that Frolic is back! Although Judith wanted a tan Whippet, Frolic chose to return as a tan Jack Russell Terrier. He returned as a male, instead of a female, but as soon as Judith saw him, she knew he was Frolic - and so did everyone who was there.

Magda and Sands

Jean Grim's husband had a herd of Holstein dairy cows. One of the cows, Magda, developed milk fever after delivering her calf. The treatment for this problem, which is not uncommon among our bovine friends, is the administration of a bottle of calcium intravenously. Somehow during the procedure the needle slipped, resulting in a large, painful swelling on the left side of Magda's neck. The next day she could barely walk and was dragging her left front leg.

That day, in a neighboring pasture, Jean Grim's twenty-five year old Arabian gelding, Sands, began moving about quite painfully and dragging his left front leg. I was working for Jean at this time, and we enjoyed talking to the animals each day. Jean had become quite skilled in communication, so she asked Sands about his sudden ailment. His reply, "The call for help went out, and I answered it."

The veterinarian came again to minister to the cow, and several days later the cow and gelding were again walking normally, giving truth to the saying "a burden shared is never too great to bear."

Departed Animals

My First Communication

I don't think I really believed anyone could actually communicate with an animal (or person) after they had died. I was fascinated by the idea, but, after all, even Houdini had not been contacted, and I would certainly imagine he would be trying hard to be heard from the grave.

The first time I contacted a departed animal, and knew it was true, I was astounded. I was at an advanced animal communications workshop conducted by Dr. Jeri Ryan, Ph.D. We participants had split into pairs and were working on problem solving.

Jane, the young woman I was sitting with made her request first. She said that she had a horse years earlier and had run out of money, so she was unable to continue to support the horse. Rather than sell Jim to someone who would pass him on, Jane had sent him to slaughter.

Jane had been tormented for years by the guilt of knowing she had destroyed Jim who had been a faithful friend and was a healthy horse that she loved. Now she wanted to know if Jim forgave her.

I listened to her and then turned to Jeri. I'm sure Jeri saw the look of confusion and disbelief on my face, but she calmly told me to close my eyes, center myself, and think the horse's name. She explained that the horse's person (Jane) and I would travel to where the horse was in the Universe. I would be able to see Jim and Jane, but Jane would see nothing.

I didn't believe this could or would happen, but I was given the description and name of the horse. I took three deep breaths to center myself and brought the horse's name into my mind three times. "Jim, Jim, Jim."

I suddenly felt as though I was flying, and I could see the stars racing by me. (*It was too much like the opening of the movie Star Wars, I could not believe what I was seeing.*) In my mind I looked to my side and there was the person, with her hand firmly holding mine. I wondered briefly how I could see this with my eyes closed, so I thought it was my imagination playing tricks on me. However, I knew we were flying through the universe - hand-in-hand.

My disbelief continued, as did our flight. Then the stars were gone, and the sky was a deep brown. Suddenly, I saw a horse! Could this be Jim? There was no horizon, or ground, or scenery, just the horse. He walked up to Jane, whose hand I was holding, and put his head against her chest, with his ears brushing her mouth. I heard him say, "I understood and thank you for what you did. I loved you so much I wouldn't have wanted to belong to anyone else."

Jane and I continued to sit together as I meditated. When she questioned me, I was able to hear her and respond easily. However, even as I answered her questions and told her what I saw, a voice in the back of my mind was berating me with, *"How dare you make things up and tell her what she wants to hear. Fraud! You have no right to do this to her. Stop now."*

But I couldn't stop. Jane was asking questions and I was telling her what was being communicated to me. Jim had been frightened by the smells of the slaughter house and the fear he felt from the other animals around him. However, after he felt the blow that ended his life, he felt serene and floated out of his body. Jim was now grateful that he was in this place, and wondered if Jane had felt him "whisk her face with his ears?"

I saw Jane smile and respond, absently caressing her cheek as she spoke, "Yes, I did feel Jim's ears whisk my face." The voice in my head was *screaming* at me to *end this farce,* but I still could not.

Jane asked what the place looked like and I described the flashing colors coming from what looked like a ball of yellow energy. It was breathtakingly beautiful, and some of the colors were new to me. They shone and danced like rays of sunshine.

I could also see a blue dome that seemed to cover an area of about three acres. I couldn't actually see anyone else in the dome, but I knew Jim was being protected and well cared for. The voice in my head was really disgusted with me by now and letting me know that *no one could believe this trash I was saying.* I felt terrible about leading her on, but, as before, I still couldn't stop myself.

Then came the big question. Jane wanted to know, "Is Sara there?"

The voice in my head was triumphant. *"Ha! You're caught now! You don't know if Sara is a horse, a goldfish, or maybe a blade of grass. Go ahead, get yourself out of this...."*

I saw a young horse whose liver chestnut coat was not a common color. She had a thin crooked blaze that ran down her face, and she stood beside Jim, and slightly behind him. Jim had been Sara's teacher.

The voice in my head was awed, *"Oh, my God!"* it said.

The happy young woman verified that this was Sara. She asked more questions and received answers that satisfied her. Then Jim backed away a few steps and I knew it was time to end the session.

Mentally I returned to this dimension, still *holding* Jane's hand. We settled in the room and I opened my eyes. Jane had tears rolling down her face, and I am sure my eyes were as big as saucers with amazement.

Jeri Ryan just smiled.

The Fluffy White Dog

Audrey Lund made an appointment to ask about her Lhasa Apsa dog, Empress. The dog's health was failing, and Audrey wanted to know what Empress had to say about how long she would be here. Empress replied she would no longer be with Audrey by the end of winter. Since this was longer than Audrey had been hoping for she felt a lot better.

Audrey then asked if I could contact the fluffy white dog that she and her mother often saw in the house. They would see it pass a doorway, but when they went to look, it was gone. Sometimes they would see it in the mirror, but on turning, there was no dog. Audrey and her mother knew the dog was not there physically, but yet they had each seen it clearly.

I asked the dog who it was, and she said her name was "Debi." Audrey had a shocked voice when she told me that one of her other dogs was named Deborah, but they called her Debi. The fluffy dog said she was there with a gray cat, but no one ever saw the cat.

When I am doing a consultation I concentrate on interpreting the message I am receiving, so I seldom have the presence to think about what may be obvious to others. If I do ask a question of the animal, it is usually for clarification in order to tell the person the information accurately.

Usually when a communication has ended I put the entire experience out of my mind. In this case, however, I found myself several months later thinking about this particular appointment and the conversation. I was wondering if there was a possible connection between the two Debi's. It is unusual for me to even think back to a consultation, let alone continue to dwell on it.

I should not have been surprised when, about three days later, Audrey called again. Empress had just died and the veterinarians could not agree on whether she had cancer or not. Audrey wanted to make an appointment to ask some questions about Empress' feelings on an autopsy, now that she was gone. She also mentioned the fluffy dog.

The dog had not been seen for some time, but it came back for several days just before Empress died. Audrey felt a dog on the bed with her. It was white and fluffy. She thought it was her dog, Nick, and as she lifted her hand to pet him, she would see Nick on the floor. When she looked back to where the fluffy dog had been there was nothing.

Recently, Audrey had been hearing two dogs jump off of her bed when none had been on it. She sensed that one was the fluffy dog, and the other was Lang, who had died a few months earlier. Once Empress died Audrey did not see the fluffy dog again, and was no longer aware of Lang.

When Audrey called for the consultation, Empress told her that an autopsy would be fine with her. She was finished with her body and felt light and wonderful without it. It was nice to be free of the pain. She said the tumor on her heart had grown rapidly and cut off her supply of oxygen. Empress also told us that Lang and Debi had come to help her with her transition, which had been most pleasant.

Empress had other messages for Audrey, and then told her that she would see the fluffy white dog again, but that did not mean Audrey would be losing another companion.

Debi then spoke to us and said that when she would be seen Empress and Lang would be with her, and also the gray cat who still remained a mystery. She was not ready to talk about him.

She also told us that although her name was the same as the other Debi in Audrey's home, their spirits were separate (this had been the source of my recent wonderings). She was a distant relative of Debi, on her mother's side, but that was the only connection. Her job in that home was as a spirit guide to the animals living there, and she was not sure why she could be seen at times.

Audrey was relieved to hear that Empress and Lang were well, and to find out more about her fluffy white visitor.

Other Experiences

Not all of my contacts with departed animals have been as dramatic as the trip I took in Jeri Ryan's workshop. Sometimes I hear myself saying something that I was not aware of until I heard myself talking. An example of this is the time I was giving a talk to a group in a small North Jersey town. A woman in the first row raised her hand and asked if it was possible to communicate with animals after they had died. I told her that it was, and told a little story about one. She started to cry, and continued to do so through the rest of the talk.

After the talk she came up to me. I asked how long her pet had been gone. She told me that her dog had died two years earlier, and I heard myself say, "Yes, he's gone, but he visits you in the room with the green chair." The little voice of doubt in my head jumped right in with, *"You'd better hope she has a green chair."*

The woman confirmed that she did have a green recliner and that was the dog's favorite place to curl up and sleep.

Many times the departed animals let me know about a special piece of furniture, mat, pillow, blanket, or some other item. There has been, "The room with the red rug," or "The house with all the big windows." There are times that a person will say that they do not have what the animal described, but the pet will be firm about it.

Once a dog talked about his blue pillow. The owner said she did not have a blue pillow in the house, but the dog stuck to his story, so I did, too. I got a call the next day. The bottom of the dog's favorite pillow was blue. It made sense that the person viewed the pillow from above and only saw the top color. The dog was closer to the ground and could see the underside color where it curled up.

One woman from Philadelphia's Main Line suburb asked where to bury her German Shepherd's ashes. I received explicit directions of, "Beneath the window with the spreading yew bushes under it, and the pine trees are across from the yews." It was the place where the dog had spent many hours lying on the cool ground while guarding the house. The ashes were buried there that day.

The Little Blond Child

One time I had a particularly hard time about another German Shepherd. The woman wanted to know which was his favorite room, favorite toy, favorite anything. I felt like I was being tested and got almost no information.

The dog repeatedly said it would come back as a guide for her daughter for fourteen years. The woman said her daughter was only three when the dog died, and the dog could not stand her, I had to be wrong. What was the dog's favorite food? Quite frankly, I couldn't tell her, and I just wanted to end the conversation.

Just as I was about to tell her that I couldn't help her, that there would be no charge, and I could give her another communicator's number, I got a mental image of a child with blond curly hair. She was wearing blue corduroy overalls. I described the child and was told she was the woman's daughter, and the child was wearing the overalls when they buried the dog.

The woman then remembered that as she and her husband went to take the dog into the veterinarian's office to be euthanized, the dog pulled back and went over to the daughter and kissed her. She remarked, "She didn't kiss us, just my daughter."

Now the dog told her story. She had come into this life to protect this child, but was not happy with her assignment. The child poked her, and pulled her tail, which annoyed her and caused her to snap. When she became quite ill and knew she was going to die, she promised the child that she would come back as a spirit guide and look after her until she was grown. The job she had come here to do would then be done....

Advice From Tara

Too many things were happening, Donna and her husband were separating after thirty years of marriage, and Donna was devastated by the death of her dog. It had been a rocky marriage, so the decision to separate did not really come as a surprise. However, the announcement that he was going to continue live in the same neighborhood so he could keep in touch with all of their old friends was unsettling.

Donna scheduled an appointment to ask if I could reach Tara, her dog. She wanted to know how Tara had felt about the problems in the marriage that led to the breakup, and to see if she had any advice to give.

We were able to contact Tara, but she would say nothing about the marriage. She did, however, have advice for Donna about getting through the pain. She said Donna used to meditate, but had not done that for some time. Tara told Donna to, "Sit in the brown chair, clear your mind, and meditate to center yourself." Donna said she did have a brown chair and that was where she used to sit to meditate. She was willing to resume that activity.

Tara then said, "Eat fruit." That sounded strange to me, but I passed the message on to Donna, who began to sob. Donna told me that she and Tara ate fruit together every morning. When Donna had calmed herself Tara sent another message. "Put the red scarf I wore around my neck into your pocketbook. When you reach for a tissue you will see it and know that I am with you." Donna confirmed that Tara had two red scarves and that she would find one for her pocketbook.

Tara's next piece of advice was, "Hold your head high and wag your tail. This was meant to be, and in two weeks you will walk out of the woods and be strong and independent." Tara also said the color yellow was very important, and there would be "petals unfolding."

Donna called with a follow-up communication two weeks later. She told me that she had begun counseling and was ready to proceed with the divorce. She was starting to feel independent, and definitely stronger emotionally. Donna had also noticed, just that day, her flowering cactus had a yellow bud that was unfolding into a beautiful flower. It had reminded her of Tara's message, which had prompted her call to me. I really appreciated the call because so often I am left hanging by not knowing the end of a story. I think this is part of the reason why I so deliberately let go of consultations when an appointment ends.

Donna has called me several times for appointments to communicate with Tara and to let her know Donna has received messages and that Tara continues to be loved and missed.

Then, my phone rang one chilly December morning, and Donna's perturbed voice was apologizing for the sudden call and inconvenience, but she had a problem. Donna had lost her car keys and had been searching for them, to no avail. She asked if Tara could help her. As Donna was finishing her sentence the word "kitchen" popped into my mind.

I told Donna that Tara said the keys were in the kitchen, but as I was telling her that I got a picture of a stuffed chair. The chair looked to be a brownish color. I asked Donna if she had a upholstered chair in her kitchen. She said she used to, but her soon-to-be-ex-husband had taken it when he left. Donna said she would start with checking the cushions of the brown chairs in her living room, and then call me back.

My phone rang again a few minutes later. This time Donna's voice was shaky, but upbeat. She had not found the keys in the stuffed chairs, so she went back into the kitchen and looked where the chair used to sit. There they were, right under a shelf where the chair had once been! The shelf the keys were under was only about four inches off the floor.

The keys had slid all the way to the rear of the shelf, and Donna was only able to find them when she was on her hands and knees, and had her head all the way to the floor. Donna started to cry and said, "As much as I loved her, I feel even closer to Tara now."

A few months after the missing keys Donna called to ask if Tara could help her find the remote control unit for her television. The answer came quickly, "On the floor, beside the bed. On the left." Donna found it there.

Another few months passed, and Donna once again lost her keys. As soon as Tara was asked she told Donna to look in her black pocketbook. Donna tipped the contents out of the pocketbook while I waited on the line. There were keys in there, but they were Donna's spare set. Donna said she wanted the others. There was the feeling of a shrug as Tara said, "Well, she has keys. I don't know where the other ones are."

Donna came across them later when she spied them sitting on her clothes drier in her basement. We guessed that Tara had not seen her lay them down.

A Promise To Return

When Stephanie Levick called I could hear the despair in her voice. She told me her horse was in a large animal hospital, and not expected to pull through. She had the horse for twenty-one years, since he was a two-year-old. Her friend, who was a veterinarian in another state, told her to call me for some input about how the horse felt.

I could tell this was an emergency call, so we skipped the formality of arranging an appointment. I asked the usual: "Please tell me the animal's name, and give me a brief physical description of him." As soon as Steph told me that she called him Dopey, I asked the horse if he minded that name. He said he did not mind because it was a fun name, and he liked to have fun. Dopey sounded sleepy, and it was difficult to communicate with him, so I asked if he was on pain killers, and found that he was.

I asked Dopey where he hurt, and I felt pressure at my navel. Steph confirmed that he had just had surgery, and that was where the incision was. It was first thought that he had colic, but a tumor was discovered that had wrapped itself around part of the intestine.

Steph asked him if he was going to live. Dopey said he did not know, but he was not afraid to die. He said he would return to her, and at first I thought he said, "In the red barn." I repeated the sentence to him before I told Steph, and he corrected me. He said, "No, it's in the barn that has the red in it."

When I reported to Steph what he had said, she told me that his stall was made of cinder blocks and wood. The cinder blocks were painted red.

Steph asked if he knew that the veterinarians would only let her visit him during certain hours during the day. He answered, "Yes, I understand. I am also aware that she talks to me each night before she goes to sleep. I appreciate this and would like if she would do it even more often." Steph said she did and she would do it more often.

Steph's voice quivered as she asked her questions, but we went on until she was satisfied that he knew she would visit him whenever she was allowed, and that he was comfortable. He said, "I know that I have given you some hellish times," but he did not express regrets, he just made the statement. Steph told me later that Dopey let her know that he did not feel that horses should be confined. He broke out of any stall that was not horse-proof, and jumped out of paddocks and pastures. Whenever he could, he took other horses with him when he escaped.

Steph called the next night to ask how Dopey felt, and I knew at once that he was not doing well. I responded with "Oh, he's having a bad time. He's in pain, and he's asking you for your help in his crossing over." He assured Steph that he was not afraid, and that he would return to her. He told her of a past life they had shared and said they would share many more.

As we talked her phone beeped with a call coming in, so Steph put me on hold. When she came back on the line she said it was the veterinarian. Dopey had taken a turn for the worse, the veterinarian wanted Steph to come at once before they put Dopey down. She asked me to tell Dopey she was on her way and to thank him for everything and for being so wonderful to her and sharing so many loving years together. She hoped he could bear the pain for another forty minutes, she was on her way. Dopey assured her that he could wait, and delivered his final message of love, "You have been a very good human. I will be back with you again." Steph called again the next day to tell me that Dopey had a peaceful end.

The following are excerpts from the letter I received from her:

"Losing him was and is extremely difficult, but knowing that he understood what was happening, and was ready to leave, and being able to really tell him how much he means to me, has made the whole experience completely different than it otherwise would have been.

"In addition, when I went to him after you and I talked, there was a different level of communication between us. In spite of all the drugs in him, and the failing state of his body, he was bright and clear, and looked right into my eyes as he communicated with me. He hugged me with his neck over and over, and rested his head on my shoulder, and I knew what he was saying as well as if he had been saying it in English."

A few weeks after Dopey's passing Steph called to ask if we could contact him. She had been having some very strange experiences and wanted to know if Dopey was behind them.

Steph had worked at a horse farm. When a mare was going to foal, or a horse was sick, Steph might have to spend the night in the barn. When she did have to, she would sleep in Dopey's stall. If Dopey was laying down in his stall when Steph came in, he would stand up until she settled in. Then he would lay down with his head near hers and his breath would blow her hair. Then he would fall asleep and snore. If Steph moved he would get up and move with her so that his face would once again be near her to blow her hair, and snore.

One night, after Dopey left her, Steph woke to the sound of Dopey's breathing. She was aware of a light that looked almost as if she was under water and looking up to the light. She opened her eyes, but the light disappeared, so she closed them again. The light returned, and she could hear the breathing again, and this time she could also smell him. She wanted to know if Dopey had come to her, or was it her imagination.

Dopey responded that he was, indeed, the visitor. He said she had cried more that day than the others, and he wanted her to know he was fine. Steph confirmed that she had cried more that day than any of the others since he had died.

The next question Steph had in mind was about a friend who also said she had a visit from Dopey. I got a picture in my mind of a room that was dark, not because of a late hour, but because of little sunlight. Steph said that was the room her friend was in when she sensed Dopey. Dopey explained that the friend had been waiting for Steph, who was late, and he wanted her to know that Steph was fine.

Steph then asked Dopey if he remembered how he used to communicate with her by sending her dreams. She asked about the time that he made her dream that she was rolling in a stall with fresh bedding in it. He said he remembered, and did she remember the dream he sent her when he made her eat something? I could see that it looked like grass or hay. Steph laughed, and told me that she certainly did remember that one. It was grass. She said that Dopey loved to eat grass so much that he wanted her to have the same experience. She had awakened that night with her hand to her mouth, reaching for the grass that was really only a dream.

Now Steph wanted to know if Dopey was behind some events that were unusual. The horse that was now in Dopey's old stall - with the red walls - was always very quiet and docile. Lately this horse had started to spill the water out of the bucket, so he could throw the bucket at Steph. (And more than once he succeeded.) The horse had never done anything like that before, but Dopey certainly had, and often.

I asked Dopey if his spirit had gone into this horse, and he said, "No, however, I can get this horse to do things for me." Steph said the horse was a follower, and would have done anything Dopey had asked him to do. Dopey said he was going to come back as a chestnut colt, but probably not this year. Steph said she was going to breed her mare and asked if Dopey would mind the mare as his mother. Dopey said he did not care as he would only be with her for a few months.

Later in the conversation Dopey told Steph that even though he always protected her, his job was to lighten her. He said he came to her during a bad time in her life, when she was down. His job was to make her laugh. Steph said he made her laugh every day for twenty-one years. He was inventive, and came up with different silly things all the time.

I just know that Dopey is not done with his shenanigans.

Gizmo

When Diana Zipper called to ask if she could contact her dog, Gizmo, who had died a few days earlier, she was so distraught that she could hardly tell me her own name. During our consultation, she was feeling somewhat better, and after our consultation Diana was breathing easier and starting to relax.

At the beginning of my conversation with Gizmo, he sent me the pain he had experienced, and then the pain left in a short time. Diana confirmed that he had been injured in that area after being stepped on by a horse, and died quickly. Most of Gizmo's emotions were surprise that this could have happened to him. He had been scolded many times, but never really believed that he was in danger.

Gizmo told Diana that he knew his life was too short, and that he would be back after the end of the summer. He had been a tri-colored Corgie, but he was going to come back as a red and white female Corgie. We found out through questions that he felt that Diana's female Corgie, Penny, was treated with more respect than he. He also felt that he wanted to be very different. Although this lifetime had been short, he had learned a lot. He did not want to change all his ways, but he definitely wanted to change his looks.

Diana said that Penny was not scolded because she did not cause the trouble that Gizmo did, and she loved him just the way he looked. She wished that he would have listened to her admonitions about the horses because then he would still be with her.

He was not daunted. He said he would not come to her until he returned as the puppy. He was just fine where he was and enjoying himself. Diana was to look for him at the end of the summer.

Diana then talked to Penny. Penny missed Gizmo, and was looking forward to his return. She was very maternal, and said she would like to have a litter of puppies and raise the new Gizmo. Diana was not sure that Penny was in good enough shape to have puppies, and I advised her to make that decision with a veterinarian instead of only on Penny's input.

Satan! Satan!

I had done several radio interviews locally over a short period of time. The stations send word to each other when they have an unusual guest. I seemed to qualify as an *unusual guest,* so I began getting calls from around the country asking if I would be on their stations by telephone hook-up. I believe that it was around the third such show that one of the interviewers asked if I could talk to animals who had already departed. I said I could, and then quickly went on to another topic.

It wasn't long after that show, I was contacted by a station in Rhode Island and I agreed to do a ten minute interview with a man and woman team of interviewers. The first question the man asked was: "I hear you can get information from departed animals. Is that true?" I responded that I usually could.

He told me he was a skeptic, but was willing to try. He gave me the name and description of a dog, and I immediately felt pain on the top of my head, on the right side.

The interviewer began talking about being on a teeter-totter with his brother, and stepping off. His brother came crashing down and was slightly hurt. He continued talking about a dog barking, a storm coming, the smell of rain in the air - things just weren't making sense. I cut in and asked what his question was to the dog. He said he wanted to know how the dog died.

I told him about the pain I had experienced, and suggested that the dog either was injured or suffered a stroke.

He just said, "Oh," so I asked what happened to the dog. The dog had been under the teeter-totter when it came down, and had been killed.

The interviewer got his thoughts together and said he had another dog, which he named and described. I felt a problem in my throat and said I believed the dog died of "something nasty in the digestive system." He responded that the dog had choked to death on a chicken bone.

The woman interviewer started to ask about animal communications, and as I was answering her questions when I heard the man's voice repeating, "Satan! Satan!" I wondered if he was calling me Satan - and hoped he wasn't, because I was going to tell him a thing or two!

I was trying to get my thoughts together, and to buy some time, I said, "I beg your pardon."

He repeated, "Satan!"

"Are you calling me Satan?" I asked, somewhat aghast.

"No!" came the frustrated response. "That's the dog's name...Satan. What did he die from?"

I said I believed he was euthanized. That's when the tirade started.

"I'll never forgive my old man for that! He was a good dog. So he crapped in the house. I was just a little kid, but I cleaned it up. Sometimes I was in school, and didn't know it happened. I know dog crap smells, but I cleaned it as soon as I got home! I loved that dog.

"I hope my mother never has bladder problems. He'll put her to sleep! I'll never...."

The phone went dead, so I hung up. A few minutes later it rang and the person who had arranged for the show was on the line. He called to explain what had happened...someone had called in to talk to me and the interviewer was so distraught by the conversation we were having, he had hung up on me by mistake.

I tried not to laugh, as the voice went on, "I have to tell you this, he's sitting in the station shaking like a leaf." He thanked me for my time and asked if I would agree to be interviewed again. I tried to be polite and said I would be happy to...somehow I don't think that will happen.

Reincarnation

The Lab Puppy

I received a call one evening from a young man who was grief stricken. A few hours earlier his dog companion had been hit by a car and killed instantly. This person was still in shock and reaching out for help. Someone had told him to call me. He did not know what to expect from me, and really wanted his dog back somehow.

The dog gave some messages of being "surprised, but well on the other side." Then he said he would return in six months as a Black Labrador puppy. He would make himself known to the young man and be recognized. He also promised to "give a sign" to him.

The dog's person told me, rather bluntly, that this was a bunch of junk. I realized this was his grief talking, as his animal companion had assured me that he was a "lovely friend." I wished him well in dealing with his grief and offered condolences on the sudden loss of his dog. When I hung the phone up I went on with my life and hoped he would do well with his.

Six months later, I received a second call from the same young man. After words of apology over our last conversation, he said he had a new Black Lab puppy. He wanted to share an amazing story with me.

Although the new puppy had some of the same characteristics as his other dog that was not enough to convince him. He told me that his wife took their other dog to work with her in a nursing home. The dog had his own name tag, but it had been lost a few days before his death. When the puppy was housebroken he was taken to the nursing home. As soon as the puppy went in, he went straight to a certain area and came out with the old dog's name tag. Did I think this was a sign? *I sure did.*

The young man thanked me and again apologized for his curt behavior six months earlier. He had been so devastated by the loss of his companion that he was unable to believe he would ever have him back. He asked to be put on my mailing list to be notified of any workshops that might be held near his home.

An Old Love

I was asked to talk to a cat to find out why her behavior had changed. Annabelle and her boyfriend David had a most interesting shop. They made and sold pyramids, and had other items of a spiritual nature. Annabelle had a cat that was always loving and friendly toward her, but suddenly the cat had started to attack her for no apparent reason.

When I asked the cat to communicate, she was reluctant to speak, but she flashed me a mental picture that told the whole story. I could see, scene by scene, settings that went back to biblical times. My first image was a very wealthy woman and her three children. She had servants to dress her, take care of the children, and do everything in her home. She was not attractive, but her hair, make-up, and clothing enhanced whatever good features she had. I knew, without being told, this was Annabelle's past life.

The next image that I received was the wealthy husband who was a politician. He gave his family everything, and took pride in his children. They were treated with respect in the community. The husband had returned to this life as David.

The next scene showed a beautiful young woman with shiny auburn hair. She stood with her two children, who were also very handsome. Their clothing was well made and fashionable, and I knew, without being told, that this young mother was the mistress of the wealthy politician. The mistress and her children would always be well cared for, but never have the status of the man's family.

Although she understood, this did not sit well with her...she was envious of his legal family. The auburn haired woman had now returned as the cat. Her memory of that life was still vivid. When she and Annabelle had lived alone she was happy to be her cat companion, but when David came into the picture, she felt that she was again being reduced to the role of *mistress*!

Annabelle said that it all made sense. The cat had really started turning on her just after David moved in. She was the most aggressive when David came home from work and greeted Annabelle before he said "Hello" to her.

The thing that Annabelle also noticed was the jewelry. David made jewelry, and sometimes gave Annabelle pieces as gifts.

When one of those gifts was laying on a counter or dresser, the cat would jump onto the furniture, stare Annabelle in the eye and use her paw to knock the piece of jewelry to the floor.

Annabelle asked what she could do to ease the situation. I suggested that David talk to the cat and tell her that he loved them both. It might be nice to greet the cat first sometimes when he came in, just to make her feel more special.

David was understanding, and had the talk with the cat. I spoke to Annabelle about a year later. The cat had responded, settled down, and stopped attacking Annabelle for a while. Months later she started again so Annabelle had a talk with her and told her that her behavior was unacceptable and to please try to be nice again.

The cat looked Annabelle straight in the eyes, turned on her heel, and marched out the door. The cat was never seen again!

Across the Prairie

During a consultation with a young woman, she asked if she and her pet had ever been together in previous lifetimes. Her pet said yes, and I began to see the scene of covered wagons slowly lumbering across the prairie. The picture formed slowly in my mind, but I could see the wagons spread out. I realized that I was looking at the wagon ahead of me, not at a team of animals pulling. I looked to my left and saw a huge ox hooked up beside me. I moved my head and eyes enough to see my own body, it was the *body of a deep red ox*. In another life the young lady had been an ox. Her current pet was the ox I could see beside her.

I told the caller, and she was delighted. She said that she passes a pasture on her way home from work where there is an ox. Whenever she sees him, she stops her car and gets out to pet and touch him. She never knew why she felt the need to do this, but now it made sense.

The Girl In The Purple Dress

Loretta Catrambone called to see if she could talk to her cat, Nick, who had lived with her for nineteen years. Our consultation unfolded in the following manner. Loretta had gone on vacation, and when she returned home she found Nick quite ill, and he died the next day. Loretta had felt guilty for several years, always wondering if she could have saved him if she was at home when his health started to decline.

When we spoke to Nick he told Loretta that it was his time to go, and he had even stayed alive for an extra three days so he would be there when she got back home. Loretta asked some other questions, and then, almost as an after thought, asked if they had been together in a previous life.

Nick said they had been together many times. He described a little girl with blond curls. She was wearing a purple velvet dress and a lacy apron over it. The little girl was sitting in a chair and holding a cat. Nick had been that cat.

The following day Loretta called again. Nick had said he wanted to come back to her soon as a cat, but she had not answered when he asked her if that would be okay. Loretta had some more questions about where to find the new Nick, and did he know she wanted him back?

Nick said he knew. He said Loretta had thought much about it the night we spoke and then made the decision the following morning. Loretta confirmed this and then gave me some additional information.

She said she had gone to a psychic years earlier with a question about whether she should go out with a certain man she knew. The psychic said that she saw the two of them together, but there was a little girl with them. She then went on to describe the same girl in the same dress that Nick had told us about.

The psychic did not know who this child was and advised Loretta to just tuck the information away and some day the answer would be revealed to her. She said the little girl was probably someone from a past life, maybe even Loretta. According to Nick the psychic was correct, the little girl had been Loretta in another life.

There was a second consultation where I received information that verified a psychic's reading. It happened when I was talking to Jim McHoul.

Jim has a Weimaraner named Margaret. During the consultation Jim asked if he and the dog had been together before in a previous life. Margaret said they had.

Jim had been a very rich lonely man. She sent me an image of a countryside that looked like England or Scotland. She said, "We lived *in a house bigger than a mansion.* Jim was very unhappy and walked a lot through the halls of the house. I was his large dog, and I accompanied him as he walked."

Jim told me the hair on the back of his neck stood up when he heard the words, *"in a house bigger than a mansion."* He had gone to a psychic one time who had told him of a past life when he was wealthy, lived *"in a house bigger than a mansion"* and was very unhappy walking through the halls.

PART II

Individuals

Porcia

My life was very different before I entered the world of animal communication. I had worked in an office for many years, while I went to the University of Pennsylvania at night to study accounting. Although I got straight A's, I chose marriage over a degree, and have never regretted that choice.

I continued to work for the same company until I was offered an early retirement package. I didn't hesitate, I took it.

A few weeks after the decision to retire I received a phone call from Jean Grim. We had both been 4H leaders over twenty years earlier. We used to see each other about once a month at leader's meetings, and just had a "Hi!" relationship.

Someone had told Jean that there was an animal communicator named Anita Curtis in the area. Jean called to ask if I was in fact the same Anita Curtis she used to know.

"Yes," I responded.

In our catching up, she told me she was managing a barn with Arabian brood mares. When she told me where it was, I was surprised to learn it was less than a mile from my home, on a street that intersects with mine. I had often walked by the barn and stopped to watch the mares and their babies in the pastures.

Jean told me that she used the services of another communicator, but that person was not taking calls for a few weeks. She wondered if I would fill in if she had any problems. I told her I would be delighted to take calls if she needed me, and immediately took the opportunity to drive over to the barn and meet the horses I had admired from the other side of the fence.

This was my formal introduction to Porcia.

Due to her Russian breeding, Porcia is large for an Arabian. Her color is referred to as flea-bitten gray, which means she is white with light brown speckles all over her body. Porcia has large, marvelous, eyes that peer into your innermost being, and when she communicates in person she stares into your eyes until she is sure you have the message she wants to convey. When I met this magnificent mare, I felt like I was standing in the shadow of greatness, but I had no idea just how deep her wisdom was.

Porcia became the mentor for all the animals. Porcia told us when changes had to be made in feed, suggested pasturing, and advised on foal raising. I had no experience with foals, but I was there when Porcia's new baby was to be led into the pasture for the first time. I started to follow Jean's instructions with me leading the mare in the front, and her guiding the baby as it followed. Porcia stopped us and told us to lead the baby and she would follow. We knew that the baby became more adventurous after a few days and wandered off, but we never thought of letting the mother follow the foal. We heeded Porcia's instructions and later in the week one person was able to lead them to and from the pasture without the usual problem of a wandering baby.

When Jean ordered supplements for the mares Porcia was consulted. From this consultation a list was made and Jean would call in the order. During one of these calls she happened to reach the president of the company. After they had completed the order, he said he wanted to tell her about some new products. The conversation became technical so I was asked to take the call, with Porcia, as the advisor.

When some products were described Porcia asked questions such as, "Does this work in the large intestine?" or "Does this have a bitter taste?" The gentleman on the phone would say, "That's a good question," and give the answer. He finally offered to send samples of the various supplements so that Porcia could see, taste, and evaluate them.

After we hung-up, I told Porcia that I was glad that she and the man on the phone understood each other, because I didn't know what they were talking about. Porcia, in her most motherly voice, said, "That's because you have not reached my level."

When the samples came Porcia checked them out, and then the order was made. Some things she chose to use at once, some to wait until the season changed, and others she felt were not needed.

Several months later the same gentleman had his daughter call to ask Porcia if she could help with a problem they were having with one of their horses. Porcia said she would be happy to help, so I asked for the name and description of the horse. As usual, I started to feel some pain in my body, and asked Porcia if she knew what to do.

I got a picture in my mind of a thick liquid that was almost white, but tinged with green. The caller said it must be mint. I advised her to look the problem up before she gave any to the horse. She called back about fifteen minutes later and read a paragraph from an equine medical book. It described the ailment, and said to give mint for it.

One evening I was with a group of friends who knew about Porcia. There was a lot of conversation going on, and background noise. One friend got me aside and asked if I would get in touch with Porcia and find out what she had to say about getting him over an addiction to caffeine. I closed my eyes, took a deep breath, and asked his question. The reply was immediate, "Eat licorice."

I remembered back over twenty years to when my husband had quit smoking. He had found a licorice product that had nicotine in it and eaten it when the craving became difficult to handle.

I figured that there was too much distraction around me and I had heard Porcia wrong, so I told my friend I would ask her later when I could be in a quiet place. Just before I fell asleep that night I remembered the request. I centered myself and asked Porcia and once again I was told, "Eat licorice."

The next morning I called my friend and gave him Porcia's advice. He said he understood, as he had studied Chinese herbs and knew anise was to calm the nerves. Since anise is an ingredient of licorice, it made sense to eat it. The problem was that my friend could not stand licorice or anise. With the information, however, he was able to find another herbal remedy that worked very nicely with his problem.

Jean was soon busy practicing communications with the mares and started getting more and more messages from them. The manifestation of her progress became apparent in an interesting manner.

One day I was at the barn alone. I began thinking about the homeopathic remedies that were being used on the mares. I was still having a difficult time grasping the concept of homeopathic remedies, although I had, more than once, seen evidence they did actually cure the malady.

About this time I was walking past Porcia's stall, deep in my thought process and absorbed in personal concentration. Suddenly, I had the feeling someone was staring at me. I looked up to find that it was Porcia. I was so deep in my own concentration, I did not realize she wanted to talk to me.

I just nodded a "Hello" as I went by, but I had a sudden change in my thoughts. I began to think about the changes that occurred when the homeopathic remedies were used. Jumpy horses immediately became calm, wounds healed in record time, just to name a few things. The whole thinking process was done in a few seconds, and I suddenly felt acceptance of homeopathy.

About this time the phone started to ring in the office, so I went in and answered it. Jean's voice came over the line to tell me that she had just received a message from Porcia saying she wanted to talk to me. Jean did not know exactly what Porcia had in mind, but it had something to do with the homeopathic remedies, and my beliefs. I told Jean that I would go and see her, but I thought Porcia had already gotten through to me. Sure enough, when I got to Porcia's stall again she just said, "Never mind."

Homeopathy played an important part in my relationship with Porcia another time.

I was going to visit Dr. Shoemaker to check the accuracy of information I received from the animals about their physical problems. Jean asked if I would ask Dr. Shoemaker a few question about homeopathic remedies for the horses. I took a tape recorder so I could bring back all the answers without taking notes.

Dr. Shoemaker said she wanted to try something with Porcia and me that she was sure would work. She got a kit of little bottles of pills, I set the recorder up, and then called Porcia into my mind. We started working.

Dr. Shoemaker handed me a bottle and told me the name of the remedy and what it was used for. I told her how I felt physically, such as an upset stomach, headache, etc. After about the third bottle she decided not to tell me what the medicine was for, just its name. As I held each bottle I experienced the symptoms of the illness that the medication was supposed to cure.

We went through the kit, bottle by bottle, and I felt headaches, stomach cramps, light headed, and so on until the last bottle was handled. I did not touch the pills, only the unopened bottles. As we continued through the kit, Porcia would tell us which horse in her barn, if any, needed the remedy. Dr. Shoemaker would then ask some questions and make the decision whether to give the dose.

There were times when Porcia's wisdom was from what we call instinct.

Jean was on mare watch when Porcia's foaling date was due. Porcia had given us the date of April 2, but although she had contractions, her baby did not actually arrive until April 9. Jean was sleeping on a cot in the office of the barn with the intercom turned on. She heard Porcia become restless and then lie down before five in the morning, and went to check on her. Sure enough the foal was on it's way.

Jean dialed my number and when I answered on the first ring I heard one word, "Now!" My eleven year old grandson, Brett was visiting with us. His mother had said he could go watch if the foal came during the weekend. I told him I would only call his name once, so when the phone rang he jumped out of bed. He had slept in his clothes and needed only to put on his shoes.

We were out of the house in two minutes and traveled the one mile in record time. When we got there the new baby, Fancy, was in the deep straw, still attached to Porcia by the umbilical cord. Porcia scrambled to her feet when she heard us come in the door, and guarded her newborn foal.

Brett climbed up on a stack of hay bales where he could see into the stall but not be in the way or be a threat to Porcia. Porcia said I could come in the stall, but only Jean was allowed to touch the baby. I thanked her and did as I was told.

Porcia then went around the stall with her head up. She sniffed the tops of the walls of the stall over and over. I asked what she was doing, and she said, "Looking for cats," and sent me a mental image of a mountain lion.

When she was satisfied that the area was free of large cats, she started to do something strange. She picked up a few pieces of straw in her mouth, and then spit them out. She walked a few paces and repeated the routine.

After watching this happen five or six times, I asked what she was doing. In an agitated tone, she said she had to get rid of the afterbirth. I told her that Jean had already done that. Porcia settled down for a few minutes, but then started picking up the straw again. I reminded her about Jean once more, but this time I showed her a picture of Jean walking out of the stall with the afterbirth in a bucket. Only then did Porcia leave the straw alone.

By that time Fancy was trying to stand, but could not get the hang of making all those legs do what she wanted them to. She flopped around the stall, under Porcia's watchful eye, from one end to the other and back again. By this time Brett could not hold his comments back anymore, and gleefully said, "Batteries not included!"

Porcia was always an excellent mother. Fancy was high spirited and could be difficult to handle, but Porcia was loving and stern with her.

When the veterinarian came several hours later to give Fancy her shots, Fancy was going to have none of that. She exploded into a dynamo of energy, running around Porcia as fast as she could. Jean and I cornered her, and then Jean called, "Porcia, please help us."

Porcia was there in a flash. She moved into the space between Jean and me and shoved her chest against Fancy, holding her tightly against the wall. She admonished Fancy to stand quietly, which she did, and the work was then done easily.

When Fancy was a yearling she enjoyed the company of one of the barn kittens. The kitten was about eight weeks old and would come to

Fancy to be licked and nuzzled. One day Fancy had licked the kitten until it was soaked and then picked it up gently by the scruff of the neck and carried it to where Porcia stood eating hay. Porcia's mind was probably solving some deep problem of the Universe, so she did not notice the wet, furry bundle that Fancy carried until the filly spit it onto the hay pile in front of her mother.

Porcia's lost her dignity and almost jumped out of her skin when the kitten landed. Jean saw the episode and almost expected Porcia to scream. Jean had a good laugh...Porcia was not amused.

One time I asked Porcia a question about something that had bothered me for some time. If it was time to bring four horses in from the pasture I would tell three of them that I would be back for them in a few minutes, and lead the first horse out. The remaining three would stand quietly. The second horse would be led away with the same result. When I was down to two horses I would explain again that I would return promptly, but this time - even if Porcia was the remaining horse - the last one left would run up and down the fence line, very upset, and calling loudly to the horse that was being led away. Why was that last horse so upset?

Porcia said "It's a horse thing." She told me to picture myself as a horse in the wild. To be alone was to be a predator's dinner, and as soon as she found herself to be the only horse in the field she became instinctively terrified and reacted out of that terror. She was in this world as a horse and she was programmed to survive. I understood.

On further reflection, I also remembered hearing Dr. Shoemaker say that acute hearing is important to the survival of prey animals. She said that if a predator does not hear a rustle in the grass he misses lunch. If the prey animal does not hear a rustle in the grass he is lunch.

Porcia carries the genes of the prey animal in her body and must act accordingly no matter what a person says to her.

It is not hard to admire this wise and instinctive mare. My feelings for her go far beyond admiration.

Junior And Tory

Jim did not begin his call with the usual questions: "How do you make an appointment?" or "What do you charge?" Instead, he told me that his wife had seen an ad I had placed. He said he had met a lady once who could communicate with animals and he believed she could do it. How could he know if I could?

I responded, "Well I don't take money in advance. That way if you are not satisfied with the answers you get, it is your option not to pay for the consultation. If you ascertain that I have, in fact, communicated with your animal and answered your questions, I will tell you the charge at the end of the appointment and you will send me a check."

This seemed to answer his question, and he made an appointment. I wondered if he would later say it wasn't his horse and not send a check, but I put my feelings aside.

At the appointed time, we completed the consultation and I told him the charges. Any feelings of apprehension on my part were totally unfounded, as he promptly send his check, and it was for double the amount it should have been.

I called to tell him his check was wrong and he told me to keep it for the next session. I felt this was going to become a regular consultation. Little did I know then that Jim and his wife Lillian would spend many hours on the phone trying to get to the root of a series of problems with their horse, Junior, trying to get him on the racetrack.

Junior is a Standardbred trotter, his 'career path' is to be a harness racer. He has a most pleasant personality, and was actually anxious to tell me his problem. He explained about his left hock. Jim confirmed that Junior was traveling in a manner that would indicate that was correct.

Junior told me about a few other minor aches and pains, some in his neck, some in his back. Then he went on to the problem that had Jim frustrated for months. Junior's left hind foot hurt. He had several veterinarians, and a large animal hospital baffled. There had been tests and X-rays but the only thing the veterinarians could agree on was "Yes, the horse is lame."

Junior knew what he needed to feel better, so over the next few months he had Jim make adjustments to his harness. The tension in the overhead check rein was changed to help his neck and back. He had Jim change the angle of his hooves. Each change would bring about improvement for a while, but then the hoof would start to sting again.

As soon as the hoof would become inflamed, his neck and back problems would also recur. To compound matters, sometimes Junior just felt like looking around instead of working. That meant he would not have a good workout, but he did not necessarily have pain.

He was still young and wanted to be silly. Deer were in the woods near the track Junior worked on, and Jim referred to them as the "aliens." Junior was more interested in making sure he was not attacked by *aliens* than he was trotting fast.

One time Jim arranged an unusual appointment. He asked if I could talk to Lillian while he worked Junior. Lillian would stand near the fence of the track and use a cordless telephone, I was home in my office, and Jim was in the cart driving Junior. Jim knew Junior made a break from a trot to a gallop when he had pain, but he wanted to know exactly where the pain was. He couldn't tell much from his position in the cart behind Junior.

Lillian called after Junior and the other horse who was being worked had been on the track for a few minutes to warm up. As they trotted I could tell when Junior pulled up beside the other horse and looked over with his ears back, to issue the challenge to trot faster.

I reported to Lillian what Junior was picturing for me. I saw Junior set his head and neck in a position to trot as fast as he could. I could hear, "One, two, one, two, one, two," faster and faster as Junior concentrated on trotting. All of a sudden I got a sharp, hot, pain in my left heel. At that instant Junior broke into a gallop and the counting in my head stopped. Jim steadied Junior, and brought him back to a walk. Now he knew that it was the hoof, not the neck, back, or harness. It was *back to the drawing board*, but at least Jim had an idea of what needed to be fixed.

Next Jim asked me to ask Junior why it hurt. Junior referred several times to "the injury." He also told us that it felt like something was inside the hoof that didn't belong there. Jim thought Junior might have abscesses, so he used a treatment to bring them to the surface. Sometimes an abscess would come out, but not always.

Junior still insisted that it was from "the injury." Jim said that he had known Junior since he was a baby and he had never been in an accident. We weren't listening closely enough; however, Junior kept repeating *injury*, not *accident*. We did not realize that we were interpreting the word incorrectly.

Jim finally called a veterinarian who worked on cows. The veterinarian said he was going to take very few X-rays, but one would be on an odd angle. When the X-ray was read it showed that the wing of the coffin bone in Junior's hoof had been broken off. It was an old injury, probably from when he was a baby, from the look of the way it had healed.

Jim gave some thought, and said that when Junior was a baby, he was always getting cast (stuck too close to the wall or under something) in his stall. When Junior was cast, he would kick and kick to try to free himself. That was how he broke the tip of the bone.

There were several options open to Jim at this time, and he chose the least drastic. A procedure was done to deaden a certain nerve to the back of the hoof. Jim waited a few days and called me to see how Junior felt. My left heel hurt. Jim retorted that it could not possibly be Junior. I backed down since I had just returned from my three mile morning walk, but I warned him that my right heel had walked as far as my left and it did not hurt.

Jim called two days later when I was sitting still, reading. My left heel started to throb immediately, and there was no doubt in my mind that Junior's left rear hoof hurt. I suggested that Jim get a hoof tester and check. He called back in a few minutes. Indeed, Junior was quite sore, the procedure had failed.

More work was done on Junior, and finally his hoof was comfortable.

Now another problem reared it's ugly head. Junior had compensated for the sore hoof for so long that his body had muscled unevenly. He was still traveling wrong. Jim worked out a plan to get Junior back in symmetrical shape, and was doing quite well.

One morning I got a call from a frustrated, angry Jim. "He's sore! I can't win! I'm getting rid of him. He'll never be any better." I always know when things are really bad. Jim does not start the conversation with "Hello," he just launches into the problem.

I stopped him cold when I told him that the left hind was still fine, his right hind hurt. Juniors shoes had just been changed, and the right hind was giving him a problem. Jim was so geared up, expecting the worst from the left that it took him a couple of minutes to absorb what I was telling him.

Finally, he settled down enough to listen. Junior told Jim what to do. He also complained that Jim had not given him his carrots...Jim promised that he would get them.

Again, the next call did not start with "Hello," but it was a good one! Jim's voice came on the phone with, "You really enjoy saving this horse's life, don't you?" The shoes were adjusted, and Junior was working well.

It didn't last. As much as Junior wanted to be a race horse, his hooves just could never hold up. Finally, Jim realized he had to give up on his dream with Junior.

Jim called me a few days later. He had been offered a fair amount of money for Junior by a man who would have used him to pull a carriage. He would have been used daily and hard.

The offer was turned down, and Junior was *given* to a good home. He would work occasionally, but usually be a pasture decoration - known in the horse world as a *meadow muffin*, and be a pet for someone's grandchildren.

Jim reminded me that I had told him in the beginning that *we had to know the right questions to ask Junior*. Part of the problem was that we had never asked him if he could recover from the injury; only if he wanted to recover.

Jim mused that animal communications was both good and bad. I asked what the bad was, and he told me that since he now knew Junior could think and feel he could not sell him to the man who wanted to buy him to work him hard, and perhaps ruin him. I let Jim know that I thought of that as the good part, not the bad!

A couple of months later Jim called again. He had changed jobs, and had a new colt to train. However, the colt was not moving quite right. At that point my left foot started to hurt and I said, "Oh no! Another left hind!" I explained where the pain was.

Jim groaned, but he knew exactly where to have the X-rays taken.

When he called again there was no "Hello." This time he started with, "You've got another good story for your book. He had a bone chip exactly where you said!"

Jim called the colt Meathead. The first few times we had consultations nothing was said by the young horse about his name. After a few calls Meathead told me that he did not like that name. He said he had been accurate about what was going on in his hoof, and wanted to be treated with more respect. He told me his name was "Tory," and he would appreciate being called by that name.

Jim assured me he would call the youngster Tory, and to this day that has been his name.

Sweet Dreams

Donna Lozito called from Long Island for a scheduled late evening appointment. I asked her the usual questions: "What is the name of your animal? Please give me a brief physical description."

Donna had already told me that she had read an article on animal communications in the July 1994 copy of the national magazine, *Equus*. After several deadend contacts, she reached Penelope Smith's office and left a message requesting information on the answering machine. She was sent a list of people Penelope had trained. My name is on that list. Since I was the first communicator she actually reached, she made an appointment at once.

When Donna gave me Sweet Dreams' description I felt like I was floating. I asked if he was on tranquilizers, or some medication that would make him feel woozy. Donna assured me that he was not on any medication.

I mentally asked permission to speak to him, and got, "Ooooookay."

I said, "Sweet Dreams, is that you?"

"Mmmmmmmm, yep."

Once again I asked Donna what he was on. She said, "Well, I did give him some _____." After a pause, "And some _____."

I asked how much, and she quietly said, "Almost a bottle of each."

I usually give a horse about three or four drops of these flower essences. Sweet Dreams was stoned out of his mind! I suggested that Donna might want to call back when Sweet Dreams was back from his trip.

Donna asked if she should change his water now. I had no idea that she lived an hour away from the stable, and therefore it did not matter that it was already past nine at night. I told her I would change it if he was my horse.

Donna told me later that when she got to the barn she couldn't find the light switch, and was dumping the water bucket outside in the darkness of the night when she heard a voice say, "Donna? Is that you? What are you doing?"

The stable manager had heard someone drive in and was investigating. Donna was too embarrassed to tell her that her horse was drunk from the drinking water that she had doctored, so she just stammered something about wanting to make sure he had fresh water.

The next night Donna called and Sweet Dreams (Sweetie) and I were able to communicate. When Donna started to describe him my left hand began to ache. I asked if he was lame on the left front, and Donna breathed a sigh of relief when she said "Yes, he is."

She told me that he had been lame for several months and the veterinarians had not been able to get him sound for longer than it took for him and Donna to have one ride. The veterinarians all suggested that she get rid of him. The kindest one told her she could turn him out to pasture on a horse farm in a southern state. The others just said to unload him and get a good horse.

Donna knows that Sweetie is her soul mate, and is not about to "get rid of him" under any circumstances. She knew that she had to save him.

The veterinarian's diagnosis was a torn suspensory ligament, but since I have made it a point not to learn anatomy, I didn't know where that was. I just knew the palm of my left hand ached, so the bottom of his left front hoof most likely also hurt.

We talked of several other things that evening, and I knew that Sweetie felt the same way about Donna as she did about him. I was concerned that, in spite of his love for her, he had a strong feeling of independence. Donna might not be experienced enough to handle him. The feeling nagged at me the next day, so I wrote her a letter to warn her to be careful.

Donna called back to say that she had ridden Sweetie with a new sense of confidence, and the good news was that the ride was wonderful. Some guinea fowl had run out on the track as she rode and everyone watching the squawking birds stopped breathing, expecting Sweetie to explode. It didn't happen. Donna felt secure and Sweetie just kept trotting as if nothing unusual had happened. Someone was video taping the whole event, and the smile on Donna's face lit up the whole screen.

The bad news was that Sweetie was lame again. As before, my left hand began to ache. I told Donna it was the bottom of the hoof. Donna said the five veterinarians claimed that the pain was higher in the leg, but two of them were going to do a nerve block the next day, and take x-rays.

When Donna called the next time she was laughing. She had watched the veterinarians work, blocking one nerve after another, and looking perplexed. They finally made the right nerve go dead, and Sweetie was sound. They still did not look happy. Donna innocently asked if they had to block the nerve that deadened the bottom of the hoof. The veterinarians said "Yes, why do you ask?"

Donna wasn't going to tell them that a woman in Pennsylvania had told her, over the phone, that the pain was in the bottom of the hoof. She just smiled and told them that she knew her horse well.

Donna's delight was short lived. She called me the next night, close to panic. Sweetie was weaving (swaying back and forth) in his stall. He had not resorted to that unhealthy habit since Donna had put him on a nutritionally sound diet. Donna said he looked wild eyed, and his ears were back, showing anger.

When I asked him what was wrong, he said his throat was swollen and hurt on the inside. He had food in front of him and could not eat. I asked what caused his throat to swell. He was furious as he started telling me about wires, electrodes, paste, and needles. I had to stop him, because I didn't understand and wanted to check with Donna. He said to tell her the soreness was from the needle in his neck. I asked Donna if she knew what he was talking about, and she said he was describing the bone scan.

I still did not understand. I had cancer and required bone scans. All I had to do was lay still on a cold table while some gadget way above me did whatever they do. I didn't have electrodes pasted to me, or a needle in my neck.

Sweetie did. Donna described the bone scan, and told me he had an IV needle in his neck the whole time it was going on. Sweetie chimed in at this point, and said that was where he hurt.

When Donna went back to the barn she felt his neck where the needle had been, and it was hot. She called the veterinarian, and when he arrived she asked about his neck. He confirmed that Sweetie had an infection, it was swollen on the inside, and he couldn't eat. Some antibiotics took care of the situation quickly.

Donna, Sweetie, and I had conversations a few times a month, and he was usually lame, and could not seem to recover fully. I wanted Donna to bring him to Dr. Judith Shoemaker, a veterinarian who practices close to me in Pennsylvania. She specialized in lameness, and in unusual cases.

Donna was getting ready to contact her in November, 1994. I was preparing for a trip to England, and was leaving the next day when Donna called, sounding more disturbed than usual. Sweetie was not exactly lame, but he wasn't right, either.

Although I was in the middle of some last minute chores, I sat down, closed my eyes, and asked Sweetie what was going on. This was to be the first of many times that I would say to Donna, "I don't believe he could tell me what he just did. See if you can check it out."

Sweetie's answer had come through with words and pictures. "I have an object in my right front hoof. It is about the size of a quarter, about one-eighth inch down from the tip of my frog [a part of a horse's hoof], to the right side of it." It was not possible to have it checked right away because he had leather pads between his hoof and his shoe. The pads would keep him from getting a bruise or injury.

Also, looking back, I think I heard some of the words, and pictured some of the rest. I don't believe he said "quarter," I think he showed me. At the time, I was clearly shocked by Sweetie's message.

Donna ignored my disbelief, and asked Sweetie what to do about the quarter. He told her not to do anything, that his body would absorb it. I said he must be wrong.

Yeah, right.

Six weeks later Donna brought Sweetie to Dr. Shoemaker. Donna picked up his X-rays just before she left New York. After the initial examination, Dr. Shoemaker put the X-rays on the light box. She went through, one by one, explaining what they showed.

I had gone to meet Donna and Sweetie when they arrived, and was looking at the x-rays but didn't understand them. I didn't remember the earlier conversation about the quarter, and wondered why Donna was getting so excited. She was pointing to something on the X-ray of his right hoof, and saying, "Anita, the quarter. The quarter."

She asked Dr. Shoemaker what the object was, and was told that it was a floating abscess. It was nothing to worry about, Sweetie's body would absorb it.

I was amazed, but that was not the end.

Dr. Shoemaker felt that Sweetie had a problem with his immune system, and wanted some blood work done before she started to treat him. A few days later Donna called to ask how he was doing.

When I posed the question, Sweetie replied, "Pretty good. My blood should be a twelve. It's six. When I am detoxed it will go quickly to nine, and then level off and climb slowly to twelve." There were no pictures this time. Just words.

Yeah, right.

I gave the disbelief statement again, and Donna said she did believe him and was going to call Dr. Shoemaker. Dr. Shoemaker got the records and said he was right on. She was impressed since she had not discussed it in front of him.

While Sweetie was visiting Pennsylvania, Donna had the opportunity to study animal communications through my workshops. She became so involved in the field that she decided to continue her studies with Penelope in California.

Sweetie remained at Dr. Shoemaker's clinic for six months. He was sound, and could have gone home in five, but this was the time Donna had scheduled to continue to advance her studies even further with Penelope. She felt more comfortable leaving him at the clinic until she got back to New York.

During his local visit, Sweetie and I enjoyed many conversations. We have continued our relationship. He never ceases to amaze me with his insight and intelligence. He can also be quite snippy with me. Once, when I was talking with Sweetie and Donna on an unscheduled call, I had to put their call on hold to take an incoming call. When I returned to them Sweetie's not-so-sweet voice filled my head with the words, "You were talking to ME!" I clearly was to show more respect.

One time in Pennsylvania, Donna was holding him while he ate grass. An Amish horse and buggy went down the road. Sweetie panicked and bolted, almost pulling Donna off her feet. Later, I asked him what happened. He casually responded, "The buggy was chasing that horse down the street!" I guess it did look that way to him.

Sweetie would also have his mellow moods and tell Donna about their past lives together. He would always help her when she was practicing animal communications with the other animals. It is so beautiful to see that kind of bond between human/animal companions.

Sweetie is healthy now, and he and Donna are enjoying their rides together.

The Briels

I met Ron and Linda Briel in 1993 when Linda's horse, Lonestar had a problem. The veterinarians said the horse was in kidney failure and if she was not put down she would shortly die a nasty death. Linda wanted to check any alternatives.

A friend told her about animal communications and she began her search to find a communicator. She contacted someone in Philadelphia and had a consultation. That communicator called me and told me that someone in my area had just spoken to her. She didn't explain the problem, just that they had horses, and I might be interested in meeting them.

I took the number, called and discovered that Linda and Ron lived only a few miles from me. I was invited to come to their house to meet them and Lonestar. Linda and I had seemed to click immediately over the phone, so I was anxious to accept the invitation.

We all chatted for a while, and then went into the barn so I could meet Lonestar. As I stood beside Lonestar I felt a pain in the vicinity of my left ovary. I told them it felt like a tube stretching inside me. The other communicator had pinpointed this as a problem area and had already given them some information, so what I was feeling confirmed her findings. Neither of us felt any pain in the kidneys. We could not say there wasn't anything wrong with them, just that we didn't feel any pain.

Linda made an appointment for a consultation with another veterinarian in Philadelphia and asked me if I would like to go along and meet her. Without hesitation, I agreed, as I was anxious to remain close to this wonderful animal.

When we got there the veterinarian palpated the mare and within minutes had found a tumor on the ovary that turned out to be the size of a small grapefruit. Lonestar was left there and had surgery to remove the tumor.

Ron, Linda, my husband, and I started to see more of each other socially, and became good friends. Linda was always looking for someone to ride with her. I had not been on a horse for years, but she loaned me her old Tennessee Walking horse, Sonny, who was "bomb proof." We had some lovely rides, and Sonny told us about his past as we rode. He could be quite caustic at times, but he also had a dry wit.

One time we rode past several farms with horses all around, but Sonny ignored them. When we got to a pasture with a horse and pony Sonny stopped and stared at the horse. The horse came right over to the ditch that ran along the fence line, and stared back. Linda said to pull Sonny away to continue the ride. I didn't want to because it was clear the Sonny and the other horse knew each other.

I have always felt it a shame not to let animals communicate with each other as long as they don't get into an argument. I have wondered what it would be like to be in a land of other species. How would I feel when I would see a human and not be allowed to converse? Instead of pulling Sonny away I asked if I could listen to the conversation. They didn't mind.

Sonny was telling the other horse that he lived in a comfortable barn, ate two meals a day plus a snack, and got to be in the pasture when ever he wanted. He didn't mind being ridden, and actually enjoyed the change of scenery.

The other horse said he just stayed in his pasture with his pony friend, but they had no shelter. He wished he could be with Sonny.

On the way home Sonny said, "Tell Linda to bring my friend home." I told him she couldn't do that. He said, "Why not? She brought me home."

I tried to explain that Linda had bought him with money. He didn't understand...or didn't want to. He insisted that if she bought him, she could buy his friend. The concept of money did not make any sense to him. I told him that to get something of value, you had to give something of value, and that was money. That was no problem to Sonny. "Let Linda give something of value, then!" Sonny never did understand why his friend could not come and live with him.

One of the things that Linda and I have in common is that Linda is a Reiki Master. Reiki is a channeling of the Universal Energy, and a wonderful healing tool. Ron has studied Reiki, as well as Shiatsu (acupressure/massage) for people and animals, and also studied equine massage. They work together on the human or animal patients with amazing results.

One day they were working on a horse and I was standing nearby. My head started to hurt across the brow, and I remarked that I had a headache. As suddenly as it started, it stopped. Then my stomach became upset. I said the headache had gone, but I was feeling nauseous. A few seconds later I was fine, and said as much.

Ron realized that I was picking up, through the horse, what he was doing. As he applied pressure to certain points of the meridian I reacted. We thought it was a pretty funny game, so I turned my back to them and continued to feel the horse's reactions.

Then we tried it on a second horse, and the sensations were the same from the pressure on the same points. We both realized that we were on to something brand new. There were a few books written on acupressure on horses, but they did not agree on all of the points. We were finding out through the horses what was right or wrong with those books. We also discovered differences between male and female, breeds of horses, and horses that were very old as opposed to younger ones.

Ron's goal is to teach the methods he uses. We have carefully documented our findings, and Ron is planning to write a book. We have worked together on many horses and ponies.

Ron has computerized, cataloged, cross referenced, and done all of the hard work on the book. I just sit with my back to them, or around a corner, and tell what I feel. Our work has been televised for the Premier Horse Network on cable TV.

One cold Sunday evening Linda called to see if I could help them with some back-up information on a horse they were going to treat.

They had been called to work on a horse that had gotten out of his stall on Friday and eaten an astonishing amount of horse feed. The veterinarian had been out several times, but it did not look good for this horse. It was the trainer of the horse who had called, as the owner was out of state, but the trainer loved the horse as if he was her own.

When Ron and Linda arrived they learned that the horse had been laying down for over a day, which is not a good sign. They immediately started their work, Linda sending the healing Reiki energy, and Ron pressing points on the meridian.

Linda took a break and called me to ask if the horse wanted to tell us anything. I felt an abdominal pain and described the location. Linda said that the horse was in a position that would make it difficult for Ron to massage that place. The horse said he needed to be rolled to reach the proper location.

He also described a place on his neck where there was a swirl of hair, and said he wanted pressure put there, too. Ron found the place, which was on a bladder meridian, and applied pressure. We don't know why he wanted it, but it was his choice, and Ron did it for him.

The horse said that he wanted to live, and wanted help. When they could do no more, Ron and Linda were invited into the trainer's house for a cup of coffee. A few minutes later someone checked the horse and said he was on his feet. He did not stay up long, but it was the first positive sign that he would recover. And recover he did!

Susan Rifkin Ajamian

I get phone calls from all over the country. The origin of an individual getting my number is often very interesting. In Susan's case, the entire initial conversation was very dynamic.

As the introductory conversation unfolded, I learned that Susan had a Bachelor's degree in Physics. Most scientific sorts want nothing to do with anything they can't relate to without documented proof. I asked her why, despite her background, she was so open to telepathy. She explained that she had first learned about animal communication from her veterinarian. "And," as she pointed out, "some of the ideas *accepted* in physics can also be pretty amazing."

A short time after our initial phone conversation, I met Susan in person through a mutual friend, and communicated with her animals for her. At that time, Susan noted that she was responsible for getting speakers for monthly educational lectures for a large horse club and she asked if I would be interested in being a speaker some month. I love to speak about animal communications to groups, and was pleased to have the opportunity.

Now, although I love to *speak*, I am quite shy about the *business* of arranging the talks. Susan, however, enjoys making connections. One thing led to another and ours has become a match made in heaven...Susan is a valued friend and my wonderful, talented publicist!

I have not been present when she makes the calls, but I can imagine what the person on the other end of the line feels when Susan says something like, "I have just read the list of speakers for your expo, and [*with an incredulous tone*] I see you don't have an animal communicator!" She then gives necessary information about me, and the next thing I know, my phone is ringing and I have a speaking engagement scheduled.

Once at the event, I must prove myself. But so far, the results have been very positive, and I am usually invited to return. This also often leads to my being approached by others in the audience to give lectures to their groups...which leads to....etc. I can generally trace much of my business back to *doors that Susan has opened for me.*

Several years ago, I told Susan that I was going to England in six weeks to see my husband's family, and wished I could give some talks while I was there. Susan called me back in two days with three contacts. There was a scheduling problem with one, but I did address two groups who were members of the British Horse Society, and got to meet some lovely people. In return for the *opened doors*, I am willing to talk to Susan's horse or two cats at any time.

Richie is a big dark bay Thoroughbred who used to give one-word answers to questions. As time went on, he started to get more talkative, and is now quite a conversationalist. He has a dry sense of humor, and mixes that with his deep sense of responsibility. There are several mares in the pasture with him, and he takes great pride in caring for them.

Susan's cats, Cassandra (Cassie), and Tigger, as well as Richie, have given us some interesting insights into the viewpoints of animals. Usually when a client schedules a consultation we talk only about important issues, and then end of the conversation. Since Susan and I spend a fair amount of time chatting with her companions, we have taken the opportunity explore broader topics.

I knew Susan took copious notes about the conversations, so when I was ready to write this chapter I asked her to provide me with some stories about her companions. She reminded me of some interesting conversations. Her animals have given us some wonderful insights into *their* viewpoints.

Richwood (Richie, Thoroughbred gelding, foaled 1979)

Richie had been on six weeks rest in his stall from a pulled tendon. We asked if he would like a tranquilizer. He declined because he did "not want to be out of his body." Instead, he asked if he could listen to classical music. He also asked for Ebbie, the barn cat, to visit and sing to him.

Later we asked Richie if Ebbie had come. He responded, "Yes, but she isn't as good as classical music."

Another time, when he was having Reiki practitioners working on him, Richie repeated to one of them who is also an animal communicator, that he would prefer classical music to the rock being played nearby on the barn radio. With this second request, arrangements were made for a spare radio to be use in the stall while Richie was laid up. He was much happier with this arrangement and appreciated the effort on his behalf.

One of the questions we had asked Richie was if there was any meaning to the swirls on a horse. (Swirls are places on a horse's face, neck, or body where the hair spreads into a circle or feathery design.) Richie told us that it was "an indication of a horse's brain wiring."

Several months later, I got an excited phone call from Susan saying that she saw an article in *EQUUS* magazine which validated what Richie was telling us. The July 1996 article quoted research from Colorado State University animal behaviorist, Temple Grandin, Ph.D., showing the correlation between swirl patterns and behavior in cattle. It is "the first scientific, documented evidence that hair [swirls] have an effect on temperament, and I am absolutely sure it applies to horses...[t]he skin and the nervous system come from the same fetal layer when the embryo develops...[w]hen the convolutions of the brain start to form, the hair patterns develop at the same time, so there is a link between hair patterns and nervous-system development." *(EQUUS, July 1996, page 15)*

In 1995 Linda Tellington-Jones published *Getting in TTouch*. She describes personality traits that can be identified just by looking at a horse's swirls. Both documentations clearly tie in with what Richie had told us. The wisdom of animals never ceases to amaze me.

Richie frequently gives specific information about Susan's riding. He is very positive in his evaluations, as he enjoys his human companion and thinks she is an excellent rider, but he also gives suggestions to help them grow as a team. He stated the purpose for their special relationship was to "help Susan with her confidence in many areas, including riding, communicating with me and general knowledge of my species."

He said he feels he has "broadened Susan's horizons and helped her to see past what she could see before. Her vision is no longer a narrow tunnel. Now she can see the countryside and not just my ears."

Susan likewise feels that through the communication channels she and Richie have developed, she has been able to help him grow in broadening his capabilities.

Richie noted that on occasion Susan would subject herself to things which pushed her almost to the limits of her confidence. Although she did okay, she would frequently forget about keeping her chin up and her back straight. He suggested, therefore, that when she does something which pushes her, that she do it for a shorter time so she can also concentrate on the physical.

He declared that sometimes she recites a checklist, and that is when she does her best riding. Debby Hadden, Susan's riding instructor, confirmed that she has given her a list about position, eyes, balanced seat bones, etc. Susan acknowledged that she does recite the list.

Richie has also become quite vocal about his equipment and preparation before a ride. He approved of being saddled with the same routine each time, and the care that was taken to smooth the hairs under the saddle. He advised Susan to switch from a snaffle bit to a Pelham for trail rides, and that the chin chain should be in the first hole if used in the riding ring, and on the third hole for trail rides.

He was in favor of all the stretching exercises except for the one where he was supposed to stretch his neck around to "smell his tail." He said "that needs to be left to flexible two year olds."

When Richie was asked why he objected to the support boots on his hind legs, he complained that the friction from the lining pulled on his leg hairs. Just after that the manufacturer announced their new boot design. The major change was the development of *"a new, more comfortable lining."*

Richie is generally very friendly with people as well as other horses. There was only one horse Susan ever saw Richie actively avoid. This was puzzling because the horse was a young friendly gelding, and not mean. When asked about this, Richie explained that the other horse had a neurological problem, something in his head did not make the right connection. Richie was afraid of him because there was no logic to his actions. This horse was later sold after he spooked badly and dragged his rider.

Richie also made clear observations about a former stable manager who caused several boarders to leave the barn because of her rages. Richie said "she has red colors out about ten inches around her, moving like fire." He continued, "She glowed in the dark with her anguish and anger."

Richie told us, "In ten years an incredible number of people will be communicating with animals." He is pleased to be a part of the cutting edge of this breakthrough. He showed me a picture that looked like cells dividing, and said, "It will help others, and others, and others."

One afternoon Susan went to catch Richie for a ride and saw that he was at the far end of the field. His pasture mate, Precious, a 28 year old mare, was standing nearby. Half-kiddingly Susan turned to her and said, "It would really be a help if you'd just call Richie over here." Precious walked a few steps, and then neighed. Richie and his pals came flying across the pasture and up to the gate. Precious turned, as if she were saying, "Well?" Susan thanked her and presented her a tasty carrot!

Cassandra and Tigger Paws (Cassie and Tigger)

Cassie and Tigger were born in May 1980. Even though they are litter mates and both spayed females, there are not many other similarities about them. Cassie is a long haired orange tabby. Tigger is a short haired tortoise shell.

Cassie has a strong personality and is very self-assured, whereas Tigger tends to blend more into the background. Once I asked them both some questions. After I had heard Cassie's answers, I asked Tigger what she thought. Cassie's voice filled my head, and I heard her say, "Oh, I'm the one who does the talking for both of us." Tigger noted that she "generally agreed with what Cassie had to say and was happy to let her do most of the talking." Since this is a typical tortoise shell trait, I was not surprised at Tigger's words.

Cassie is becoming more absent minded lately. Tigger is coming out of her shell and talking more, it has taken a long time for that to happen.

Susan called me one day and said Cassie was holding her ear at a strange angle. I said it felt like a swelling, possibly an abscess. Although I never diagnose, I will mention what it feels like - I try to make that clear. Susan whisked Cassie off to the veterinarian and it was confirmed that she had an abscess.

Another time, Cassie told me that when her cystitis flared up she got a "twitchy" feeling on the left side of her bladder area. Susan gave Cassie a Reiki treatment, along with her prescription. During a flare-up, she could feel the twitching on Cassie's left side below her tail.

Susan asked Cassie why cats purr. She responded there is a flap in her throat at the root of the tongue. When she feels euphoric her body relaxes, breathing in and out creates the purr.

Cassie is no longer very outgoing, but she purred up a storm when she met Susan's two-year-old nephew, Nathan, whose parents and doctors were concerned about his not talking. We asked Cassie why she was so taken with him. She said "he talks to me with pictures of toys and food. He is very bright and likes cats!"

Tigger had been on a new prescription for about three months . She said she was pleased that she had gained weight. (Her initial weight loss and elevated heart rate were the symptom that initiated their veterinarian to diagnose her hyperthyroidism.) Tigger said it was a status symbol. "Skinny cats eat out of trash cans," she arrogantly stated. (This now *proud lady* was not reminded that she had once been a *barn kitty* who was adopted to be a house cat.)

Tigger showed me a double image of Cassie to illustrate that she was "not completely in her body." Tigger said, "It is only Cassie's mental capacity, her body is healthy." She continued in stating it could mostly be reversed, and "...that which was laying dormant can be reactivated by Cassie's interaction with someone in particular."

When Cassie seemed improved we asked Tigger again, and this time she showed a double image that was not as wide apart as before - her way of indicating that Cassie was more tuned in to her surroundings.

We have asked the cats about their food and prescribed medicines. Cassie said her new food gave her more energy, and in fact at the age of fifteen-plus she was regularly begging for someone to play with her. Tigger said her medicine for her hyperthyroidism made her feel calmer and she did not have a fluttering in her throat anymore. As earlier noted, Tigger's heart rate had been significantly elevated before the medication.

I continue to enjoy communicating with Susan's animals and do so frequently. In the meantime, Susan has also come to several workshops and has learned how to talk to them herself. Quite a step for a *scientific type*!

BB

In February 1994 I was going to California to take an advanced study course with Penelope Smith. At the time I was working with Jean Grim at a stable near my Pennsylvania home. I was enjoying my early retirement opportunity which enabled me to pursue a new career with animal communications.

I always find that life has a way of taking care of itself, if you are open and listening to opportunities. Jean, whom I had known for some twenty five years had recently re-contacted me when she became aware that I did animal communications. Since she was looking for a communicator, this seemed an ideal time to renew an acquaintance.

Again fate stepped in when the two girls who had been working at the barn suddenly quit. Jean was stuck, and although I did not want to start a career of mucking stalls at the age of fifty eight, I said I would help until they got someone else to take the job.

The job was only for a few hours in the morning, and an hour or so in the evening, so it did not interfere with my communications at first. When I started to get very busy at all different hours, and found myself trying to juggle consultations with shoveling horse manure, I knew I had to leave the job with the horses. At this point, the interim job had stretched to a year and a half, and I had grown to love the beautiful mares. Jean was delighted to have a built-in animal communicator on the premises, and I know our parting was difficult for her, as it was for me because of the way I felt about the mares. A year later Jean came to work in my office as my assistant.

Change happened rather quickly as I had to take off for six days because of the scheduled workshop. One of the mares that I was particularly close to was due to foal. The day before I left I asked the mare when she was going to have her baby. She said, "Tuesday five."

That made no sense to me, it was now the end of January, but February 5 was on Saturday, so I asked if she meant Tuesday at five o'clock. She repeated her "Tuesday five" answer. When I pressed her for more information she started to get exasperated, and then refused to communicate with me any more. She looked so huge and uncomfortable that I felt sorry for her, so I gave her a kiss on her nose and a scratch on her withers, and let her be.

On Saturday, the fifth of February, I woke up in my room in California and knew the baby had arrived. As soon as possible, I called my husband in Pennsylvania to ask. He said Jean had called him to say that when she arrived at the barn at seven in the morning she found the perfect bay filly standing beside her mother. The mare had given no signs the night before that she would deliver the foal, so nobody was on mare watch. The veterinarian was called to give the baby her first shots, and she estimated the birth of the filly to be about three in the morning.

I was not to be home until late Tuesday, and I couldn't wait to see the new arrival. My plane was one of the last to land that day in one of the many storms we had that awful winter. I struggled to make my way to rescue my four-wheel-drive vehicle in the parking lot.

The normal hour-long trip from the airport took almost four hours in the sleet, ice, and wind. I don't like flying, and was exhausted from my tension during the flight, followed by the additional tension of the drive home. As a result, I slept in Wednesday and didn't get to the stable until late morning.

I went straight to the foaling stall and when I opened the door the mare, Briana, proudly stepped aside to let me see her baby. I took one look at the spindly legged, skinny foal with the beautiful bright eyes, and I was in love with her.

Her fuzzy coat was solid brown with no white at all. Her black mane, forelock, and tail were soft, curly, and short. All four legs had black stockings almost up to the knee, or hock. She bounced over to me and put her head up, and I kissed the perfect little muzzle that was in my face. She had a funny habit of sticking her tongue out of the side of her mouth and sucking on it with a slurppy sound.

Most children who love horses have a favorite color. They will tell you of their dream black stallion, white Arabian, or golden Palomino. You seldom hear of a bay as their fantasy horse. When I was a child I always daydreamed of owning a bay. It was a bay Quarter Horse that I dreamed of, not an Arabian, but here was this beautiful bay baby...with rather a stocky build for an Arabian. I fell in love with her!

We had promised Briana that we would give her owner a list of names that she would like for her baby, and Legend's Desire was the first on her list. The filly's sire was Bask Legend, and Briana though that would be a lovely name for her. The owner accepted it, and that was how she was registered.

The name, however, was just too long to use all the time, so we needed a barn name. We were trying to figure out what to call her, and *oooing*, and *aaahing* all over her, when the mare in the next stall offered a suggestion.

The other mare was Porcia. She and Briana had been enemies since they met. The problem was that each mare thought of herself as the lead mare. If they had been in a wild herd they would have had an all out battle to earn that title. As soon as they met, even though they were in captivity, the instinct loomed in their brains, and they hated each other.

Porcia who had been quietly enduring all this fuss over her rival's offspring, decided she had enough of it. Frequently an Arabian filly is named Bint, which means *daughter of*. Porcia told Jean, "I'll tell you what to call her. Call her Bint Bitch."

Jean stifled a laugh, but she decided that it could just as well have been, Bint Briana, so she shortened it to BB, and everyone seemed satisfied.

With all the excitement of the filly's birth, the trip to California, and the terrible winter, I was still hadn't found a resolution for BB's birth date of February 5. It finally dawned on me that was the anniversary date of my mother's death in 1981. I knew there was more to it than just that date, but I seemed to be only getting insights a little at a time.

The next time the light went on in my mind was when I thought about my mother's name, Beatrice. When she was a child she was called Beebee. I had not named the filly BB, but it was quite a coincidence.

I began to look for other coincidences. BB's habit of sucking her tongue came to mind. My mother smoked about four packs of cigarettes each day, so she always had something sticking out of her mouth. *Could it be her?...No...it was too bizarre.*

I loved to kiss the foal's little whiskery face, and BB was usually ready for me to kiss her. If anyone else tried to kiss the filly, she would nip at them. My mother always wanted me to kiss or hug her, but she smelled so much like a dirty ashtray that I kept my distance.

When my mother died, we had a lot of unfinished business remaining in many areas of our relationship. For years after her death, strange things happened around my house. I finally had someone come and ask her to leave.

After that we had no more unusual events or sightings. Now there was this filly who was so beautiful that I had to love her. *Was there a deeper connection?...No...other people had these experiences with reincarnation...but it couldn't happen to me.*

I still couldn't figure out, "Tuesday five." One day I was being still and meditating, and I thought of the date of my mother's death. Another lightbulb. It had been *Tuesday, February fifth.* Tuesday five.

Still thinking that this could never happen to me, I decided to reassure myself by asking some questions of a pendent. I took my trusty 3/8 lead fishing sinker down from it's hook and asked if I should ask some questions. The sinker began swinging so fast that it began to bounce and I almost dropped it. The answer was "Yes." I was to ask questions.

I decided to cut right to the quick and started with, "Is BB the reincarnation of my mother?"

"Yes."

I had to steady my hand, but I asked, "Does she know who I am?"

"No."

"Does she feel that I am special to her?"

"Yes."

"Is she here to work out karma from our lives together?"

"Yes."

"Am I the one who will help her through it?"

"No." That was a shock! I went through a series of people and kept getting negative responses. Finally I asked if it was Briana, and the answer was "Yes."

WOW!

BB's owner was thinking of sending her out of state to be trained in a few months. The thought of seeing her go off in a trailer, and not being able to see her almost daily brought tears to my eyes. I thought she was beautiful in every way, but actually she was not a good prospect to show as a baby. She was a bit too stocky for an Arabian, and due to her short neck, she did not hold her head the way Arabian show judges liked. Further, her tail did not go high when she ran, in typical Arabian fashion. She was more like a quarter horse than an Arab. Her owner was not pleased with her. I knew I wanted to buy her, so everyday I went into her stall and said, "Look *ugly*. It's only for a while, so look *ugly*."

Finally, Jean approached BB's owner and told him I loved the filly, and would like to buy her. He named a low price that I could afford, and I wrote the check. BB was mine. I went straight into her stall and said, "You can look beautiful now."

I bought the filly in December, but did not want to bring her home right away. For one thing, we had just installed electric fence, and BB had never been exposed to that before. There were also several other logistical situations that needed to be resolved. We do not keep our horses locked in stalls. The doors are open so they can come and go as they please. Colonel was used to this arrangement, but BB was young and also used to being kept in at night. I was afraid that this would be confusing.

Then there was Colonel, the lonely old gelding. BB had never seen a male horse before, and I didn't know how she would react. Actually, I was just afraid to bring her home, and was making all kinds of excuses. I told Jean that I was scared that BB would miss her mother, or get frightened and bolt through the electric fence. Jean admitted that she had some of the same concerns.

As we sat in the office at the barn, and discussed the problem, I suddenly had BB's mother's voice in my head. Briana told me to bring her along for a week when I brought BB home and she would get her settled in. It was a beautiful and simple plan - I wished I had thought of it.

I asked the mare's owner if I could borrow Briana for a week, and told him why. He said it was no problem.

The big day came. We had fenced off part of the pasture for Colonel, but he could come up to the fence to sniff and talk to BB and Briana when they arrived. We were going to keep him separate for almost a week.

Jean was waiting at the barn when my friends Ron and Linda Briel arrived with their horse trailer. My husband and I were all set for the big move. I explained what was going to happen to BB and gave her a few drops of a Flower Essence Remedy to calm her. I considered taking some also since it is also safe for humans, but I figured I would be okay without it.

I held BB beside the trailer while Briana walked in. I told her once more where she was going. She spread all four legs out and said, "No!"

Briana whinnied an encouraging blast that reverberated through the metal trailer and flowed out into the countryside. BB said, "That's not my mommie," and held her ground.

My husband, Vic, and I have hauled horses for years in trucks or trailers, and always managed to load even the most reluctant of them. Here stood this baby, less than a year old, legs spread, head up, and defiant.

It came to the point where she would either have to be whipped, or we would have to take several days to train her to load. I decided on another alternative. Walk her home. However, I promised her that I would not let her win another battle.

It was a strange scene as we walked the mile. Vic and I each had a lead shank on BB, and were walking on either side of her. Jean was leading Briana behind us. Ron was walking in the middle of the road to slow traffic, and Linda was driving the pick-up that pulled the trailer. I felt like all we needed was to be singing, "I love a parade."

BB was having the time of her life, and had no fear of the few cars that passed us. When we got home and put the mare and filly into the pasture Colonel raced to greet them. He was in love. Within two days he was allowed in with BB and her mother and ready to protect them both with his life.

At the end of the week Briana told me she was ready to go home, and that BB would be fine. She had showed her the fence and water trough, and knew Colonel would take good care of her. Linda brought the trailer over, and BB watched her mother walk calmly into it. They whinnied to each other, and then the trailer left. BB whinnied and ran in circles for about five minutes, and then went to Colonel for comfort. They talked for a few minutes, and then she put her head down and nibbled grass. Over the next few hours she looked a few times to where she had last seen her mother, but Colonel stayed right beside her, and she accepted the parting. I cried for two days.

BB has been a delight to train. She is so used to communicating that we explain what we are going to do, promise her a carrot for being good, and get on with the work. She has learned everything quickly and one day will pull a cart. I have been guilty of spoiling her some, but she is usually well behaved.

BB doesn't know that horses don't usually talk to people, so she just jabbers away to us. One day she was standing by the water trough. She whinnied to Vic to get his attention. Vic asked what she wanted, and clearly heard, "water" in his mind. He told her that she could not need water since he had filled the trough less than an hour earlier.

As Vic turned to walk away BB whinnied again. When Vic asked again what she wanted, the word "water" was repeated. He again started to walk away, but thought he might as well check the trough. When he did he found that BB had pulled the plug out and the trough was dry.

I was beginning to doubt that my fishing sinker had been right about Briana being the one to help BB work through her karma. After Briana went home I thought that was the end of their time together, although I know better than to doubt what I am told.

Briana became quite ill with a condition known as founder. Founder is a disease that a horse gets for a variety of reasons. It generally causes lameness. It can also come from a thyroid condition. None of the typical conditions for founder were present in Briana's case, and there was no reason for it to happen, but she foundered.

The condition is not generally life threatening. But since Briana's case was so unique and severe her owner was considering putting her down. Ron and Linda Briel stepped in and asked if they could take her and work their healing modalities on her.

By the time Ron and Linda had Briana sound and well again her owner had decided to get rid of some of his horses. Ron and Linda now needed space for another horse who had health problems, so Briana came to me.

Ron and Linda brought her in their trailer and got here about two minutes before I returned home from an errand. They put her in a stall, and opened the top of the Dutch door so BB and Colonel could greet her.

As I arrived they were all touching noses and making deep, loving sounds. BB began to run back and forth saying, "Thank you," over and over. We let Briana out and they all stood by each other for the rest of the day.

The next morning BB was more subdued. It seemed that Mommy was not pleased with how spoiled BB was becoming and put some manners on her. BB did not whinny to me to complain that I was late. In fact she came in last for breakfast. I asked her if Mommy had scolded her, and heard a quiet, "Yes, but I don't want to talk about it." Being a typical youngster, a couple of hours later BB was back to her bubbly self.

BB is not only our precious girl, she has added the healing that I never thought could happen in my life.

I am pleased to report, that as I write these pages, Colonel, BB and Briana continue to live happily together at our home. The Colonel gets older, BB grows more adult, and Briana enjoys good health once again. Briana has said she would like to have another baby, but this is not a decision I am at liberty to make. She is still owned by someone else, although we feel she is one of our own.

Epilogue

Each day brings me a new and exciting adventure. My life is never routine. Animal communication is sometimes funny and lighthearted, sometimes deeply sad, but always different.

I am very grateful to be a part of giving voices to animals. It is such a thrill to get a letter such as the one from Pat Carnesi that said "...You told me something was hurting my dog. You thought it was her tooth or something in her ear. Well, I started rubbing her ear and mouth. I felt a lump by her mouth. My dog is a Mastiff. She had cancer last year and she was operated on. It was all gone, but I check her all the time to make sure no bumps are back, and I would have never felt the one on her cheek if it was not for you."

Susan Ajamian's horse, Richie, told me that animal communication will become common within ten years. It is a privilege to be part of the movement that will bring greater understanding and connection between our beloved animal companions and ourselves.

Penelope Smith's pioneer teachings started many of us on the path of using the skills within us to understand our critter friends, and I love to teach others her method of the basic skills of communication. I have also developed a second workshop that is more advanced.

I have the hope of teaching people to communicate with people who are non-verbal. I have mapped out a program that I believe is workable, based on Penelope's procedure for animals. Perhaps that will be the direction I will take when everyone is in communication with their pets and I am no longer needed to interpret.

In the meantime, love your animal companions - and talk to them - know they understand.

P.S.

The lovely Arabian mare, Porcia, passed away April 22, 1998 after a long illness. She asked to be remembered for her wisdom, humor, and courage - not for her pain.

Porcia will always live in the hearts of those who loved her.

Bibliography

Penelope Smith, Animal Communications Specialist, offers books, audio and video tapes, a quarterly journal (Species Link), lectures and workshops on the subject of interspecies telepathic communications, intelligence and awareness, healing and counselling. For a free catalogue of Penelope Smith's books, tapes, lectures and courses, write to Pegasus Publications, P.O. 1060, Point Reyes, CA 94956 USA, or call (415) 663-1247. To order books and tapes with your credit card, call 1-800-356-9315 (US and Canada).

Penelope Smith is the world's leading teacher of basic and advanced interspecies telepathic communication, and has helped launch the careers of numerous professional animal communicators.

Anita Curtis, has an extensive private animal communication practice. Consultations are available by appointment and can be scheduled by calling (610) 327-3820. She also offers lectures, one and two day workshops and a one day advanced workshop. Anita has a newsletter, which she sends free to all her clients. To order additional copies of Animal Wisdom: Communications With Animals, send $11.95 (US) plus $2.00 s&h (PA residents only $14.79, includes sales tax) check or money order only, to Anita Curtis, P.O. Box 182, Gilbertsville PA 19525-0182. Quantity discounts available.

Further Suggested Reading:

How to Hear the Animals, Anita Curtis.

Animal Talk: Interspecies Telepathic Communications, Penelope Smith, Pegasus Publications.

Animals...Our Return To Wholeness, Penelope Smith, Pegasus Publications.

Bach Flower Remedies To The Rescue, Gregory Vlamis, Healing Arts Press.

Diviner's Handbook: A Guide To The Timeless Art, Tom Graves, Destiny Books.

Dr. Pitcarian's Complete Guide to Natural Health for Dogs & Cats, Richard Pitcarian D.V.M., Ph.D. and Susan Pitcarian, Rodale Press.
Flower Essence Repertory, Patricia Kaminski & Richard Kats, Flower Essence Society.

Getting in TTouch: Understand And Influence Your Horse's Personality, Linda Tellington-Jones with Sybil Taylor, Trafalgar Square Publishing.

Healing Your Horse, Snader, Willoughby, Khalsa, Denega, Basko, Howell Book House.

Kinship With All Life, H. Allen Boone, Harper Collins.

Love, Miracles, And Animal Healing, Allen M. Schoen, D.V.M. & Pam Proctor, Simon & Schuster.

Species Link Newsletter, Penelope Smith, Pegasus Publications.

Tellington TTouch (The), Linda Tellington-Jones with Sybil Taylor, Viking.

thinking in pictures, and other reports from my life with autism, Temple Grandin, Doubleday.

Treatment Of Horses By Homeopathy, George Macleod, M.R.C.V.S., D.V.S.M., Daniel Co., Ltd

HOW TO HEAR THE ANIMALS

HOW TO HEAR THE ANIMALS

ANITA CURTIS

TABLE OF CONTENTS

INTRODUCTION

One day a friend suggested I write a book on how to communicate with animals. I told her my animal communication practice was very busy, my husband's health problems occupied much of my time, and I wouldn't know where to begin writing a "how to" book. She said, "You teach workshops, you should be able to write about it."

I still had doubts, so I meditated and got in touch with the lovely and intelligent Arabian mare, Porcia, who was a "force" behind my book, *Animal Wisdom - Communications With Animals*. I asked, "Porcia, if I write a book will you help me?" I received, "Sure. No problem. The book will be called *How To Hear The Animals*." In my mind I could instantly see the format of the book and the cover. It all happened so quickly that it took my breath away. Porcia added, "It is time. Humans must learn to hear us, and you must help. The communications between people and animals must grow stronger. This bond with animals will help people advance on their path toward spiritual enlightenment."

The rest of the work was not as light and airy. Porcia became ill and could not spend as much time and energy as she had before, so it was up to my human friends and me to do the tasks involved with putting a book together. When I asked her, Porcia was able to give me some advice, such as how to list the meditations in the table of contents. I did not want to offend any of the animals by putting cats before dogs, or horses first, and so on. Porcia advised, "Alphabetical. We will be fine with that."

I asked Susan Ajamian to read what I had written to make sure it was clear. Susan and I live in different states, so after she reviewed the manuscript, we would spend many hours on the phone, sometimes deciding on a single word.

INTRODUCTION

We got through it with our friendship still intact!

Stacey Small of Equilite, Inc. volunteered her business partner's expertise on flower essences. The last chapter of this book is written by Celeste Caruso. I often suggest the use of flower essences to address emotional attitudes, problems, and fears that affect the behavior of animals. Quite often I take them myself.

Jean Grim and Carol Heringslake made my life easier as they kept the office running smoothly while I was working on the book. That's not always an easy task for many calls come in to the office daily about lost, stolen, and sick animals. These calls cannot wait. Jean and Carol had to work hard to schedule emergency appointments and still give me time to write this book. When Porcia said, "You must help," she involved not just me, but a whole group of us. We are all pleased to be part of sharing with you, "How To Hear The Animals."

TACT - THE ANIMAL COMMUNICATOR'S TASK

Once you work the exercises in this book and practice communicating with animals, it will be natural for you to want to help the animal companions of your friends and family. Be very careful of how you give information to people!!!! It is wonderful and exciting to be able to hear the animals. However it is vital to remember that the most challenging part of your roll as "interpreter" is to carefully choose the words you use to communicate to your fellow humans! Listen to the animal and then present the message in a tactful, gentle way. To say, "Your lost pet is dead in a ditch, covered with flies, and he suffered for hours," is to give a horrifying picture the pet owner will carry forever. Think before you talk!

When I deal with a pet who has died, whether traumatically or peacefully, I ask the pet if his spirit is at peace, if he left his body quickly and without much pain, and I ask other questions that will let the owner know her friend is well. I usually ask if the animal has returned to visit his person, and if so, to describe the surroundings. I often get information such as: "In the room with the green chair," "In the room where the windows open out," etc.

Many professional animal communicators have extensive training in social work and counseling. If you plan to convey messages from animals to people I strongly recommend you attend some courses on counseling. There are some developed specifically for the issues encountered when communicating between pets and their people.

Judy Szela, M.S., M.Ed, is a professional counselor. She and I have developed a one-day workshop that will help the communicator listen and help the grieving pet owner.

Empathy is extremely important. Most of us are devastated by bad news concerning our pets, so you must be able to react sympathetically to the person's pain. You must have an appropriate vocabulary so you can carefully choose words that are tactful, while still truthful.

You are entrusted with the responsibility of telling the truth. It is your job to present the truth in a manner that is for the greater good of all involved.

Ethics

Our job is to interpret. We are not to judge either the animal or the person involved in the communication. There are some situations we might like to see changed, but we must recognize the feelings of others and respect them. Be humble, and move on with your own life.

We must never gossip about communications we have received. Confidentiality is a must!

DESCRIBING, NOT DIAGNOSING OR PRESCRIBING

Before you practice the exercises and meditations, it is important to know a few pitfalls you need to avoid, and some helpful steps you need to take before communicating with people.

Many concerned owners will ask for your help and advice about the physical problems of their animals. **It is the veterinarian's job to diagnose an illness or injury.** For you to do so is considered practicing medicine without a license, which is against the law. What I do is feel the animal's pain in a corresponding part of my body. I then describe the location and sensation, but I do not give my personal theories about the cause. Some examples are:

APPROPRIATE TO SAY:
Soreness in the spine near the withers
He feels crampy in the area of the navel
A metallic taste in the mouth
His left foreleg hurts below the knee
He feels cold and achy

DO NOT SAY
It is the 7th cervical vertebra
He has colic
He has a problem with his liver
He has a broken bone
He has a fever

You can help by asking an animal when he started to feel bad, or how he thinks he was injured. You can also say the animal thinks a chiropractic adjustment would make him feel better, and describe the location of the discomfort. **Prescribing pharmaceuticals is a job only for veterinarians.** However, you can help the animal by describing to the owner how a medication makes the animal feel. This can help identify effective treatments and also alert owners to problems. If an animal says the medication makes him feel worse advise the owner to call the veterinarian immediately. It is wise to suggest checking with the pharmacist if there are any questions about dosages or differences in pills.

I have had animals tell me they want to be given "the brown liquid" or "the green pill" because it made them feel better. When you pass this information to the owners make sure you let them know you are repeating the animal's request, and they should consult their veterinarian. I often say, "I am not a veterinarian, nor is your pet. Please ask your veterinarian about this." If the veterinarian does not believe in animal communications it may be a good idea to just ask if the "brown liquid" would be a good choice for treatment.

It is best to recommend that an owner ask the veterinarian's advice before giving her animal non-prescription, or OTC's (over-the-counter) medications. Many drugs that are safe for humans are harmful, or even deadly to some animals, such as Tylenol for cats. Even a safe OTC may not mix well with prescribed medications the animal is taking.

Sometimes it is appropriate to give the owner the name and phone number of a resource person so she can get information about a particular product in order to discuss it with the veterinarian.

Although homeopathics are sold over the counter, they are powerful medications and should be handled with knowledge and respect. Using the wrong one can make a problem worse. If the veterinarian is open to animal communications, he or she may have questions to ask the animals about what makes them feel better or worse. This will help the veterinarian pinpoint the appropriate remedy.

PURPOSE

How many times have you said, "I wish I knew what my pet wants"? Know you can talk to the animals, just like you talk to your friends. You may also wonder if they understand (they do), but at least you know you have tried to send a message. However, getting an answer is the amazing part of communicating with the animals.

How To Hear The Animals is designed to help people study the art of communicating with animals. It is not a substitute for attending a workshop. When people attend an animal communication workshop they find the energy from the other class members helps with their focusing and learning. I have participated in several basic and advanced workshops with Penelope Smith and Jeri Ryan, as well as courses on counseling and teaching. In addition, I have spent countless hours practicing. This book is designed to help you practice. It is the first step in learning to communicate more with animals. There is much to learn and experience and *How To Hear The Animals* is just one of many tools.

Telepathy is defined as "communication of one mind with another at a distance." Animals regularly use telepathy to communicate with each other. Early Man also communicated telepathically before his vocal cords developed enough for him to speak. We still have the "wiring" to use telepathy, but now that we have language, we use it instead of thought transference. However, we still often have telepathic experiences in our lives, but dismiss them as being coincidence or weird. For example, you may think of someone you have not talked to for a long time, and then hear from that person. When the person was thinking about calling you, you received the telepathic thought. Other examples are when you can finish a sentence for someone, or "just know" the outcome of a story you are hearing. Again, telepathy is involved, and we do it often.

MATERIALS

This workbook is part of a kit, which includes a notebook, pen, an envelope with colored cards to be used with the warm-up exercises, and an audio tape of the meditation on *"Meditation on Being an Animal."* The tape also serves as an example of how to record other meditations from the workbook.

For most of the exercises and the series of meditations which I have designed to help you become in tune with different animals, you will need a tape recorder and several blank 60 minute tapes. A watch or clock with a sweep second hand will help you time the pauses while recording.

For the meditations on animals you know, you will need photographs of the animals your partner knows so you can obtain verification of the information you receive.

Relax and enjoy the experience.

HOW TO DO THE EXERCISES

To do the meditations effectively, you should listen to them with your eyes closed. I recommend someone read the meditation pages to you, or better yet, tape record the material and play it back to yourself in a quiet, comfortable place where there are no distractions. You can pick and choose the exercises you want to tape within the chapter, but do as many as you can to experience as much variety as possible. I have outlined various meditations to help you become in tune with different animals. Some of these animals will be ones that are, or have been in your life. Others will be animals you have seen but do not know on a personal level. Once you have done an exercise you can tape over it and do another.

Do one tape as a test. I strongly suggest you speak slowly as you tape. I have put pauses throughout the meditations to allow you time to form images. After you work with the first tape you will know how to adjust the lengths of the pauses to suit yourself. The meditations are spaced so you can note changes to the length of time you pause, or change anything you would like. Once you adjust the reading for your own comfort you can make tapes of several meditations and work through them.

Record the tapes in the same chapter order as the meditations, as each level of work is based upon the meditation preceding it.

Some of the exercises are designed to work with a partner. You can pre-record the meditation, and then you and your partner can listen together.

Many people worry about communications received being "just my imagination." You need an imagination to be able to do this work. If you cannot imagine you can do something, you will not be able to do it! Working with another person offers an opportunity for verification of the information you receive. You will soon learn to trust your abilities.

HOW TO DO THE EXERCISES

Communicate with as many animals as possible. The more you do, the more you will believe that you are actually hearing them. As a matter of ethics, before talking to any animal be sure you always ask permission from the animal's person. There are times when you communicate with the animals that they send you analogies, symbols, or metaphors. You may not understand their messages; however, the animal's person usually will understand the meaning. If not, ask the animal to explain.

Some of the meditations mention blending with the animal's aura. Auras are the emanations, or energy fields, that surround all living organisms. Auras extend out from and surround the body.

When you have finished each meditation it is a good idea to record your thoughts, observations, feelings and impressions in a notebook or in your workbook.

RECOGNIZING PREVIOUS ANIMAL COMMUNICATIONS

We have all communicated with animals in some way at some time. You may have suddenly decided to check your pet's water bowl and found it to be empty. As soon as you filled it your animal companion proceeded to take a drink. Your pet probably sent you the message that his bowl needed water.

Even before I knew about telepathic animal communication I found my dogs always seemed to know when I was going to bathe them. I was very careful to gather the dog's towels and shampoo when they were not watching. However, when bath time came the dogs inevitably knew about it and were hiding. Now I realize that as I collected the bath materials I had pictures in my mind of what I was going to do, and the dogs "read" the pictures. Of course that was a communication, even though I did not intend it to be one.

This chapter provides exercises to help you remember the times when you communicated with animals, even if you were not aware of those times. You can do these exercises alone if necessary; however, if you are working with a partner, either in person or by phone, first write your answers in a notebook, then take turns answering the questions at the end of this chapter. The events you remember may have happened recently or years ago; it does not matter. What is important is that you become aware of the fact that you have communicated with animals before.

You and your partner must listen to each other's stories without comments or judgments. Listening is good practice for the times when you communicate with the animals, as you will have to listen without interruption.

RECOGNIZING PREVIOUS COMMUNICATIONS

Exercise:

1. Describe a time when you felt pleased with the actions of an animal because he understood what you wanted him to do, and he did it.

2. Describe a time when you understood what your animal wanted you to do, or not do.

3. Describe a time when your animal companion knew you were sad, happy, excited, fearful, etc. and shared your emotion, or tried to help you.

4. Describe a time you were able to tell the emotions of your animal friend, and knew why he felt that way.

5. Describe a time you realized you and your animal companion had communicated.

WARM-UP EXERCISES:
Exercise #1

You will need at least one other person to work with you on this exercise. I recommend doing this in person, but it can be done by telephone.

This kit contains an envelope with colored cards in it. One person will hold the envelope and be the transmitter, the other person or persons will receive the images. Each person should center herself by closing her eyes, taking three deep breaths, and imagining a large door at the base of her breastbone. See the door open wide. The information will travel through this door from the transmitter to the receiver.

When both parties are ready they will open their eyes. The transmitter with the envelope will take one of the cards half way out of the envelope, but hold it so the receiver cannot see it. The transmitter will then stare at the card and note its color. The transmitter will silently say the color and push the word and thought of the color through her open door, toward the receiver or receivers. After the color is sent, the transmitter must be sure to let the transmission color go instead of letting the transmission linger in her mind. Hanging on to it could inhibit the receiver from getting it. Let the receiver know when you have sent the thought by a nod, or by saying "OK."

The receiver will accept this information through her open door and see, hear, or get the feeling of the color received and tell the transmitter the color that came through.

Exercise #2

You will need to work with a partner for this exercise. One person will be the transmitter, the other person or persons will receive the images. Do the exercise several times, taking turns in being transmitter or receiver. Tape record the following meditation, or have a third person read it to you.

WARM-UP EXERCISES

The person recording or reading should decide on a color to use before starting the exercise.

Reader says:

"Sit in a comfortable position. Do not cross your legs, feet, or arms. Close your eyes and take three deep breaths to center and relax yourself *PAUSE FOR 20 SECONDS* Allow yourself to breathe deeply and normally. Feel your brow relax. *PAUSE FOR 10 SECONDS* Relax your jaw. *PAUSE FOR 10 SECONDS* Feel your shoulders loosen and drop. *PAUSE FOR 10 SECONDS* Feel your stomach muscles relax. *PAUSE FOR 10 SECONDS* Allow the relaxation to flow down your body. As you breathe out ask that any negative energy be removed. Let the negative thoughts flow down through your body, out through your feet, and be sent into the universe to be reversed into positive energy. Know, as you breathe in, this is a gentle and loving way to communicate telepathically.

"Imagine you have a door at the base of your breastbone. *PAUSE FOR 5 SECONDS* Open this door wide to send and receive the communication.

Transmitter, see the color _____ in your mind. Is it bright? Is it dull? Does it sparkle? As you see this _____ color in your mind, form an image of an object in this color. *PAUSE FOR 30 SECONDS* Use the first image that comes to your mind. Now, push this image through the open door toward the receiver. Let it go completely.

Receiver, accept this image through the open door and see, or get the feeling of the image. Stick with the first image you receive. *PAUSE FOR 20 SECONDS*

When you are ready, open your eyes and compare the information received with that which was sent."

These exercises are favorites of many people because they learn to trust themselves. Since you are practicing with another person you can verify that you successfully communicated telepathically with each other.

Some people prefer to have the information sent from the forehead, or third eye. That technique is also very effective; however, I learned to do this using the base of the breast bone and find it works well either way. In order to keep the exercise simple, I will just describe it one way, but do whatever is best for you.

MEDITATION ON BEING AN ANIMAL

This meditation is recorded on the tape that is enclosed with your kit. You can listen to it as an model of how to tape your meditations.

In this exercise you will ask an animal to come to you to help you. Accept the animal who volunteers to teach you even if you would have chosen another. You may feel several animals during the exercise, and that is fine. You may feel as if you are one with the animal, or as if you are watching it. Either is correct.

Sit in a comfortable position in a quiet place. Do not cross your legs, feet, or arms. Close your eyes and take three deep breaths to center and relax yourself. *PAUSE FOR 20 SECONDS* Now breathe deeply and normally. Feel your brow relax. *PAUSE FOR 10 SECONDS* Relax your jaw. *PAUSE FOR 10 SECONDS* Feel your shoulders loosen and drop. *PAUSE FOR 10 SECONDS* Feel your stomach muscles relax. *PAUSE FOR 10 SECONDS* Allow the relaxation to flow down your body. Let any negative thoughts flow down through your body, out through your feet, and be sent into the universe to be reversed into positive energy. Know, as you breathe in, this is a gentle and loving way to get to know an animal.

Imagine you have a door at the base of your breastbone. *PAUSE FOR 5 SECONDS* Allow the door to open wide to allow the communication to flow from the animal to you.

While in this relaxed state of deep breathing let an animal to come to be your guide and teacher. Ask this animal to appear to you. *PAUSE FOR 45 SECONDS* Observe it. See its color or colors and texture of the fur, feathers, scales, or skin. *PAUSE 10 SECONDS*

Note how the animal carries its head and body. *PAUSE 10 SECONDS*

Allow yourself to become close to this animal. Imagine yourself standing next to - but not touching - the animal, looking out in the same direction. Be close enough to have your auras blend into each other. *PAUSE FOR 10 SECONDS* In your mind gently slide sideways into the animal's body and become one with it. *PAUSE FOR 30 SECONDS* Look through the eyes. Are they on the front of the face or the side? *PAUSE FOR 10 SECONDS* Feel the ears. Do they move? *PAUSE FOR 10 SECONDS* Feel the shape, height, and weight of the body from the end of your nose or beak to the tip of your tail. *PAUSE FOR 20 SECONDS* Feel the surface of the ground beneath your paws, hooves, or body, or the water around you, or a branch in your talons. *PAUSE FOR 10 SECONDS* Move around in this body. Are you powerful, petite, graceful, or awkward? *PAUSE FOR 20 SECONDS*

MEDITATION ON BEING AN ANIMAL

Smell the odors and fragrances around you *PAUSE FOR 10 SECONDS* Listen to the sounds. *PAUSE FOR 15 SECONDS*

Are you male or female? *PAUSE FOR 10 SECONDS* Do you have young? *PAUSE FOR 5 SECONDS* Do you raise and nurture your young with your mate? *PAUSE FOR 10 SECONDS*

Move into a territory that is unfamiliar to you. *PAUSE FOR 20 SECONDS* Sense danger. See a predator stalking you. *PAUSE FOR 20 SECONDS* Is this a human or other animal? *PAUSE FOR 5 SECONDS* What is your reaction - flee or fight? *PAUSE FOR 2 SECONDS* Decide to flee. Race to a safe place. *PAUSE FOR 10 SECONDS* Look around. Know you are unharmed. *PAUSE FOR 10 SECONDS*

Go to an area where you are comfortable. *PAUSE FOR 10 SECONDS* See food that you like and can have. *PAUSE FOR 5 SECONDS* Eat and enjoy the food. *PAUSE FOR 10 SECONDS* Groom your-self. *PAUSE FOR 10 SECONDS* Feel content and tired. Find a safe place to rest, and settle down. Sleep. *PAUSE FOR 30 SECONDS* Awaken stretch, and yawn. *PAUSE FOR 10 SECONDS* Feel joyous and play.   *PAUSE FOR 15 SECONDS*   See humans approaching you. Do you want to contact them? Is there any message you would give them?   *PAUSE FOR 20 SECONDS*   See another animal of your species. Who would you prefer to be with?   *PAUSE FOR 5 SECONDS*

Take a deep breath and slowly slide back into your own human body.   *PAUSE FOR 15 SECONDS*   Look at the animal teacher and see how you feel about it now. *PAUSE FOR 10 SECONDS*   Thank it for its help and guidance.   *PAUSE FOR 10 SECONDS*

Return now to your physical surroundings, open your eyes and take one more deep breath.

MEDITATION ON BEING A BIRD OF PREY

I often see red tailed hawks circling over our property. I asked one to help me, and he agreed. I also heard the voice of a turkey vulture who wanted to share his ideas. He told me to consider his value in the balance of nature. He said people considered him repulsive and ugly, but without his work of cleaning up, we would have a pretty ugly place to live. He also mentioned that he was as regal as the hawk in flight.

Sit in a comfortable position. Do not cross your legs, feet, or arms. Close your eyes and take three deep breaths. *PAUSE FOR 20 SECONDS* Allow yourself to breathe deeply and normally. Feel your brow relax *PAUSE FOR 10 SECONDS* Relax your jaw. *PAUSE FOR 10 SECONDS* Feel your shoulders loosen and drop. *PAUSE FOR 10 SECONDS* Feel your stomach muscles relax. *PAUSE FOR 10 SECONDS* Allow the relaxation to flow down your body. As you breathe out ask that any negative energy be removed. Negative thoughts can flow down through your body, out through your feet, and be released into the universe to be reversed into positive energy. Know, as you breathe in, this is a gentle and loving way to get to know an animal.

Imagine you have a door at the base of your breastbone. *PAUSE FOR 5 SECONDS* Allow the door to open wide to allow the communication to flow from the bird to you.

MEDITATION ON BEING A BIRD OF PREY

Continue to breathe deeply, and now ask a large bird to be your guide and teacher and to help you. Ask this bird to appear to you. *PAUSE FOR 30 SECONDS* Observe the bird. See the bird's color or colors, and the design on the feathers. *PAUSE FOR 10 SECONDS* See the beak and eyes. *PAUSE FOR 10 SECONDS*

Allow yourself to mentally become close to this bird. In your mind image yourself next to the bird, facing in the same direction. Be so close that, even though you are not touching, your auras blend. Slide sideways and gently become one with the bird. *PAUSE FOR 20 SECONDS*

Look through your eyes. *PAUSE FOR 20 SECONDS* Feel the weight of your body. *PAUSE FOR 20 SECONDS* Are you male or female? *PAUSE FOR 5 SECONDS* Sit on a branch and feel your feet wrapped around it. *PAUSE 10 SECONDS* Move around on the branch and experience how it feels. *PAUSE FOR 20 SECONDS* Push off the branch and launch yourself into the air. Flap your wings and fly to another branch. *PAUSE FOR 20 SECONDS*

Be aware of the smells around you. *PAUSE FOR 10 SECONDS* Listen to sounds, and notice how acute your hearing is. *PAUSE FOR 10 SECONDS*

Fly high enough to feel an air thermal and slow your wings as you float in the air. *PAUSE FOR 10 SECONDS*

MEDITATION ON BEING A BIRD OF PREY

Look down to the ground for rodents or other food. *PAUSE FOR 10 SECONDS* See a mouse running in the grass. *PAUSE FOR 5 SECONDS* Swoop down to catch the mouse. *PAUSE FOR 5 SECONDS* The mouse ducks into a hole. Fly to a branch and sit and watch the hole for a while to see if the mouse will come out again. *PAUSE FOR 10 SECONDS* Decide the mouse will not come out and fly off. *PAUSE FOR 10 SECONDS*

Find your mate and gather nesting materials. *PAUSE FOR 20 SECONDS* Go to the place you will build your nest and you and your mate arrange the materials to begin the nest. *PAUSE FOR 10 SECONDS* See other birds looking at your nest location. Warn them to go elsewhere. *PAUSE FOR 10 SECONDS*

Fly to a safe place high in a tree. *PAUSE FOR 10 SECONDS* See some humans below you. How do you feel about them? Is there any message you would like to give them? *PAUSE FOR 20 SECONDS*

Take a deep breath and move back to your own human body. *PAUSE FOR 20 SECONDS* Look at the bird and see how you feel now. *PAUSE FOR 10 SECONDS* Thank the bird for the help and guidance. *PAUSE FOR 20 SECONDS*

Return now to your physical surrounding, open your eyes and take one more deep breath.

MEDITATION ON BEING A SMALL BIRD

I asked the birds who eat from the feeders in my yard to help with this meditation, and to tell me what they want humans to know about them. They instructed me to look carefully at their nests and be aware of the construction. When I had done this they told me they do not teach their young to build nests. They give instructions about flying and eating, but nest building is a knowledge that is a part of their being. I said the nests were a work of art, and asked if they were proud of their ability to build them. The answer I received was that pride did not matter. It was just part of being who they are. One chickadee's advice was, "Forget your pride. Just DO!"

A few days later the birds told me to walk beside the forsythias and look around. As I walked I saw several praying mantis egg cases on the branches. Once again I was able to marvel at the way they were made and the fact that they were on the southeast side of the shrubs, insuring their exposure to the sunlight that would make them hatch.

Sit in a comfortable position. Do not cross your legs, feet, or arms. Close your eyes and take three deep breaths. *PAUSE FOR 20 SECONDS* Allow yourself to breathe deeply and normally. Feel your brow relax. *PAUSE FOR 10 SECONDS* Relax your jaw. *PAUSE FOR 10 SECONDS* Feel your shoulders loosen and drop. *PAUSE FOR 10 SECONDS* Feel your stomach muscles relax. *PAUSE FOR 10 SECONDS* Allow the relaxation to flow down your body. As you breathe out ask that any negative energy be removed.

MEDITATION ON BEING A SMALL BIRD

Negative thoughts can flow down through your body, out through your feet, and be released into the universe to be reversed into positive energy. Know, as you breathe in, this is a gentle and loving way to get to know an animal.

Imagine you have a door at the base of your breastbone. *PAUSE FOR 5 SECONDS* Allow the door to open wide to allow the communication to flow from the bird to you.

Continue to breathe deeply, and now ask a small bird to be your guide and teacher and to help you. Ask this bird to appear to you. *PAUSE FOR 30 SECONDS* Observe the bird. See the bird's color or colors, and the design on the feathers. *PAUSE FOR 10 SECONDS* See the beak and eyes. *PAUSE FOR 10 SECONDS*

Allow yourself to mentally become close to this bird. In your mind imagine yourself next to the bird, facing the same direction. Be so close that, even though you are not touching, your auras blend. Slide sideways and gently become one with the bird. *PAUSE FOR 20 SECONDS*

Look through your eyes. *PAUSE FOR 20 SECONDS* Feel the weight of your body. *PAUSE FOR 20 SECONDS* Are you male or female? *PAUSE FOR 5 SECONDS* Sit on a branch and feel your feet wrapped around it. *PAUSE 10 SECONDS* Move around on the branch and experience

MEDITATION ON BEING A SMALL BIRD

how it feels.   *PAUSE FOR 20 SECONDS*   Flap your wings and fly to another branch.   *PAUSE FOR 20 SECONDS*   Sing your song to the world.   *PAUSE FOR 20 SECONDS*

Be aware of the smells around you.   *PAUSE FOR 10 SECONDS*   Listen to sounds, and notice how acute your hearing is.   *PAUSE FOR 10 SECONDS*   Fly to a bird feeder and experience eating your favorite food.   *PAUSE FOR 30 SECONDS*   Wipe your beak on the feeder.   *PAUSE FOR 10 SECONDS*   Fly to a branch and groom your feathers.   *PAUSE FOR 20 SECONDS*

Fly and land on the ground under the bird feeder. Hop around eating the seeds in the grass   *PAUSE FOR 20 SECONDS*   See a cat stalking you. Fly away.   *PAUSE FOR 5 SECONDS*   Sit in the tree and watch the cat go away. Make sure he is gone.   *PAUSE FOR 10 SECONDS*

Find   your   mate   and   gather   nesting materials.   *PAUSE FOR 20 SECONDS*   Go to the place you will build your nest and you and your mate arrange the materials to begin the nest.   *PAUSE FOR 10 SECONDS*   See other birds looking at your nest location. Warn them to go elsewhere.   *PAUSE FOR 10 SECONDS*

MEDITATION ON BEING A SMALL BIRD

Fly onto a telephone wire with a group of other birds of your kind. How do you interact with them?   *PAUSE FOR 20 SECONDS*   See the shadow of a hawk circling over all the birds.   *PAUSE FOR 2 SECONDS*   Sound an alarm and fly away with the others.

Fly to a safe place high in a tree.   *PAUSE FOR 10 SECONDS*   See some humans below you. How do you feel about them? Is there any message you would like to give them?   *PAUSE FOR 20 SECONDS*

Take a deep breath and move back to your own human body.   *PAUSE FOR 20 SECONDS*   Look at the bird and see how you feel.   *PAUSE FOR 10 SECONDS*

Thank the bird for the help and guidance.   *PAUSE FOR 20 SECONDS*

Return now to your physical surrounding, open your eyes and take one more deep breath.

MEDITATION ON BEING A CAT

I was helped with this meditation by Susan Ajamian's 18 year old orange tabby cat, Cassandra. My son Joe's cat, Seven, was also invited to join in the exercise. Seven wanted to stress the importance of being a serious hunter who helps keep the rodent and bird population in balance. Cassandra said her duties were more of a spiritual nature that only highly evolved beings were permitted to do.

Sit in a comfortable position. Do not cross your legs, feet, or arms. Close your eyes and take three deep breaths. *PAUSE FOR 20 SECONDS* Allow yourself to breathe deeply and normally. Feel your brow relax. *PAUSE FOR 10 SECONDS* Relax your jaw. *PAUSE FOR 10 SECONDS* Feel your shoulders loosen and drop. *PAUSE FOR 10 SECONDS* Feel your stomach muscles relax. *PAUSE FOR 10 SECONDS* Allow the relaxation to flow down your body. As you breathe out ask that any negative energy be removed. Let any negative thoughts flow down through your body, out through your feet, and be released into the universe to be reversed into positive energy. Know, as you breathe in, this is a gentle and loving way to get to know an animal.

Imagine you have a door at the base of your breastbone. *PAUSE FOR 5 SECONDS* Allow the door to open wide to allow the communication to flow from the cat to you.

Continue to breathe deeply, and now ask a domestic cat to be your guide and teacher and to help you. Ask this cat to appear to you. *PAUSE FOR 30 SECONDS* Observe the cat. See the cat's color or colors, and length of the coat. Note the condition of the coat, whether shiny or dull. *PAUSE FOR 10 SECONDS* See the nose and eyes. *PAUSE FOR 10 SECONDS*

Allow yourself to mentally become close to this cat. In your mind imagine yourself next to the cat, facing the same direction. Be so close that, even though you are not touching, your auras blend. Slide sideways and gently become one with the cat. *PAUSE FOR 20 SECONDS* Look through your eyes. *PAUSE FOR 20 SECONDS* Feel your ears, and listen through them. Feel how they can move and rotate. *PAUSE FOR 20 SECONDS* Feel the weight of your body. *PAUSE FOR 20 SECONDS* Feel your paws on the surface on which you stand. Do you feel grass, or carpet, or bare floor? Move around and experience how it feels. *PAUSE FOR 20 SECONDS* Sit down. *PAUSE FOR 20 SECONDS* Let your legs inch forward and lie down. Tuck your front paws into your chest. *PAUSE FOR 20 SECONDS* Stand up again and stretch. *PAUSE FOR 20 SECONDS* Feel your tail, and make it move.

Be aware of the aromas around you. *PAUSE FOR 10 SECONDS* Listen to sounds, and notice how acute your hearing is. *PAUSE FOR 10 SECONDS* Experience eating your favorite food. *PAUSE FOR 30 SECONDS* Clean your whiskers. *PAUSE FOR 10 SECONDS* Sharpen your claws on tree bark. *PAUSE FOR 20 SECONDS* Lick your fur. *PAUSE FOR 20 SECONDS*

Lie in a ray of sun. *PAUSE FOR 30 SECONDS* See the tail of a mouse moving invitingly behind a chair. *PAUSE FOR 20 SECONDS* Realize that it was a string. *PAUSE 5 SECONDS* Go outside through a cat door, and stalk a bird patiently. *PAUSE FOR 20 SECONDS* See the bird fly away before you can reach it. *PAUSE FOR 20 SECONDS* See a dog bearing down on you. Run to a tree. *PAUSE FOR 5 SECONDS* Climb the tree and watch the dog go away. Make sure he is gone. *PAUSE FOR 10 SECONDS* Climb down and go home. *PAUSE FOR 20 SECONDS* See someone you love sitting in a chair and feel the need to sit in her lap. *PAUSE FOR 10 SECONDS* Jump onto her lap and turn a few times and lie down. *PAUSE FOR 10 SECONDS* Feel yourself purring. *PAUSE FOR 20 SECONDS*

While you are with your favorite person, see another cat coming toward you. What do you do? *PAUSE FOR 20 SECONDS* Now you feel hungry. Ask the person to give you food. Rub your body around her legs. *PAUSE FOR 20 SECONDS* Does the person understand you? What does she do? *PAUSE FOR 10 SECONDS.*

Take a deep breath and move back to your own human body. *PAUSE FOR 20 SECONDS* Look at the cat and see how you feel now. *PAUSE FOR 10 SECONDS* Thank the cat for the help and guidance. *PAUSE FOR 20 SECONDS*

Return now to your physical surrounding, open your eyes and take one more deep breath.

MEDITATION ON BEING A DOG

My Black Labrador Retriever, Derby, helped with this meditation. Derby wants to stress the jobs that dogs perform. He said to include service, companionship as well as protection. He told me too, that most dogs are very instinctive and find chasing and hunting exhilarating.

Sit in a comfortable position. Do not cross your legs, feet, or arms. Close your eyes and take three deep breaths to center and relax yourself. *PAUSE FOR 20 SECONDS* Allow yourself to breathe deeply and normally. Feel your brow relax. *PAUSE FOR 10 SECONDS* Relax your jaw. *PAUSE FOR 10 SECONDS* Feel your shoulders loosen and drop. *PAUSE FOR 10 SECONDS* Feel your stomach muscles relax. *PAUSE FOR 10 SECONDS* Allow the relaxation to flow down your body. As you breathe out ask that any negative energy be removed. Let the negative thoughts flow down through your body, out through your feet, and be released into the universe to be reversed into positive energy. Know, as you breathe in, this is a gentle and loving way to get to know an animal.

Imagine you have a door at the base of your breastbone. *PAUSE FOR 5 SECONDS* Allow the door to open wide to allow the communication to flow from the dog to you.

MEDITATION ON BEING A DOG

Continue to breathe deeply, and now ask a dog to be your guide and teacher and to help you. Ask this dog to appear to you. *PAUSE FOR 30 SECONDS* Observe the dog. See the dog's color or colors, and the length of the coat. Note the condition of the coat, whether shiny or dull. *PAUSE FOR 10 SECONDS* See the nose and eyes. *PAUSE FOR 10 SECONDS*

Allow yourself to mentally become close to this dog. In your mind imagine yourself next to the dog, facing the same direction. Be so close that, even though you are not touching, your auras blend. Slide sideways and gently become one with the dog. *PAUSE FOR 20 SECONDS* Look through your eyes. *PAUSE FOR 20 SECONDS* Feel your ears, and listen through them. Feel how they can move. *PAUSE FOR 20 SECONDS* Feel the weight of your body. *PAUSE FOR 20 SECONDS* Are you male or female? *PAUSE FOR 5 SECONDS*

Feel your paws on the surface on which you stand. Do you feel grass, or carpet, or floor? Move around and experience how it feels. *PAUSE FOR 20* Sit down. *PAUSE FOR 20 SECONDS* Let your legs inch forward and lie down. *PAUSE FOR 20 SECONDS* Stand up again and stretch. *PAUSE FOR 20 SECONDS* Feel content and happy and wag your tail.

Be aware of the aromas around you. *PAUSE FOR*

MEDITATION ON BEING A DOG

10 SECONDS Listen to sounds, and notice how acute your hearing is. *PAUSE FOR 10 SECONDS* Experience eating your favorite food. *PAUSE FOR 30 SECONDS* See if there is any more food that you missed. *PAUSE FOR 20 SECONDS* Lick your chops. *PAUSE FOR 10 SECONDS*

Go outside and look around. *PAUSE FOR 20 SECONDS* Is it your job to protect? Do you see or hear anything that is threatening? *PAUSE FOR 20 SECONDS* See some bushes. There is movement behind them. Feel the hackles rise on the back of your neck. Growl. *PAUSE FOR 10 SECONDS* An evil man is about to run into your house and attack your person. *PAUSE FOR 20 SECONDS* Become aware this was actually nothing but a shadow and your person is safe. *PAUSE FOR 20 SECONDS* Look around again. See a stick, pick it up and toss it in the air. *PAUSE FOR 10 SECONDS* Run and play with the stick. *PAUSE FOR 30 SECONDS*

See, smell, or sense an animal near you that you would like to chase. Is it large or small? Is it a bird? *PAUSE FOR 10 SECONDS* What do you do? Point? stalk? or dash after it? *PAUSE FOR 20 SECONDS* Try to catch it. *PAUSE FOR 30 SECONDS* The animal eludes you and you will have to try another time. Stop and rest. *PAUSE FOR 20 SECONDS*

Return to your house and ask to be let indoors. *PAUSE 10 SECONDS* See your favorite person sit in a chair. Go and sit touching her. *PAUSE FOR 20 SECONDS* Ask to be petted and scratched. *PAUSE FOR 10 SECONDS* While you are with your favorite person see another dog coming toward you. How do you feel? What do you do? *PAUSE FOR 10 SECONDS* Now you would like a dog treat. Ask the person to give you one. *PAUSE FOR 20 SECONDS* Does the person understand you? What does she do? *PAUSE FOR 10 SECONDS.*

Take a deep breath and move back to your own human body. *PAUSE FOR 20 SECONDS* Look at the dog and see how you feel now. *PAUSE FOR 10 SECONDS*

Thank the dog for the help and guidance. *PAUSE FOR 10 SECONDS*

Return now to your physical surrounding, open your eyes and take one more deep breath.

MEDITATION ON BEING A FISH

This meditation can be done over and over and be different each time. It can range from a small fish in an aquarium to a huge whale in the ocean. When I asked some of the fish for help I was introduced to a group in a large tank. They told me to note how busy they were keeping their environment clean and neat. Several picked up pebbles, cleaned them, and spit them back out on the colorful floor of the tank. Others picked at the plants or cleared algae from the glass. They knew their jobs, and did them willingly.

Sit in a comfortable position. Do not cross your legs, feet, or arms. Close your eyes and take three deep breaths. *PAUSE FOR 20 SECONDS*   Allow yourself to breathe deeply and normally. Feel your brow relax.   *PAUSE FOR 10 SECONDS*   Relax your jaw. *PAUSE FOR 10 SECONDS*   Feel your shoulders loosen and drop.   *PAUSE FOR 10 SECONDS*   Feel your stomach muscles relax.   *PAUSE FOR 10 SECONDS*   Allow the relaxation to flow down your body. As you breathe out ask that any negative energy be removed. Negative thoughts can flow down through your body, out through your feet, and be released into the universe to be reversed into positive energy. Know, as you breathe in, this is a gentle and loving way to get to know an animal.

Imagine you have a door at the base of your breastbone. *PAUSE FOR 5 SECONDS*   Allow the door to open wide to allow the communication to flow from the fish to you.

MEDITATION ON BEING A FISH

Continue to breathe deeply, and now ask a fish to be your guide and teacher and to help you. Ask this fish to appear to you. *PAUSE FOR 30 SECONDS* Observe the fish. See the fish's colors, and the design on the scales. *PAUSE FOR 10 SECONDS* See the fins and tail. *PAUSE FOR 10 SECONDS*

Allow yourself to mentally become close to this fish. In your mind imagine yourself next to the fish, facing the same direction, and floating gently in the water. Be so close that, even though you are not touching, your auras blend. Slide sideways and gently become one with the fish. *PAUSE FOR 20 SECONDS.*

Look through your eyes. *PAUSE FOR 10 SECONDS* Feel the water passing through your gills. *PAUSE FOR 10 SECONDS* Are you male or female? *PAUSE FOR 5 SECONDS* How long is your body? *PAUSE FOR 10 SECONDS* Feel and taste the water that surrounds you. Is it warm or cold? Salt or fresh? *PAUSE FOR 10 SECONDS*

Swim with a school of other fish of your kind. *PAUSE FOR 10 SECONDS* Play a game of fish tag. *PAUSE FOR 10 SECONDS* Seek food and eat. *PAUSE FOR 20 SECONDS* Swim quickly, straight up and through the surface of the water. Turn and splash back into it, nose first. *PAUSE FOR 10*

MEDITATION ON BEING A FISH

SECONDS   Swim to the bottom of your territory and look around.   *PAUSE FOR 10 SECONDS*   Is the water clear or murky?   *PAUSE FOR 5 SECONDS*   Are there plants, rocks, fish? Swim among them.   *PAUSE FOR 10 SECONDS*

See a large predator coming after you. Feel the fear and speed away.   *PAUSE FOR 5 SECONDS*   Go to a place where you will be safe and rest.   *PAUSE FOR 10 SECONDS*

See a group of humans in a boat, on the land, or swimming toward you.   *PAUSE FOR 5 SECONDS*   How do you feel about them?   *PAUSE FOR 10 SECONDS*   Is there anything you would like to tell them?   *PAUSE FOR 20 SECONDS*

Take a deep breath and move back to your own human body.   *PAUSE FOR 10 SECONDS*   Look at the fish and see how you feel now.   *PAUSE FOR 10 SECONDS*   Thank the fish for the guidance.   *PAUSE FOR 10 SECONDS*

Return now to your physical surrounding, open your eyes and take one more deep breath.

MEDITATION ON BEING A HORSE

The two horses who helped me with this meditation were Porcia, an Arabian mare, and my 33 year old gelding Colonel. Porcia wanted people to be aware of her spirituality and wisdom. Colonel, however, had been abused and wanted to give people a message about being compassionate toward animals. As you do the meditation, feel the spirit and depth of these wonderful beings, and also know the fear and helplessness they can suffer.

Sit in a comfortable position. Do not cross your legs, feet, or arms. Close your eyes and take three deep breaths to center and relax yourself. *PAUSE FOR 20 SECONDS* Allow yourself to breathe deeply and normally. Feel your brow relax. *PAUSE FOR 10 SECONDS* Relax your jaw. *PAUSE FOR 10 SECONDS* Feel your shoulders loosen and drop. *PAUSE FOR 10 SECONDS* Feel your stomach muscles relax. *PAUSE FOR 10 SECONDS* Allow the relaxation to flow down your body. As you breathe out ask that any negative energy be removed. Let the negative thoughts flow down through your body, out through your feet, and be released into the universe to be reversed into positive energy. Know, as you breathe in, this is a gentle and loving way to get to know an animal.

Imagine you have a door at the base of your breastbone. *PAUSE FOR 5 SECONDS* Allow the door to open wide to allow the communication to flow from the horse to you.

Continue to breathe deeply, and now ask a horse to be your guide and teacher and to help you. Ask this horse to appear to you. *PAUSE FOR 30 SECONDS* Observe the horse. See the horse's color or colors. Note the condition of the coat, whether shiny or dull. *PAUSE FOR 10 SECONDS* Is there a long or short mane and tail? *PAUSE FOR 10 SECONDS*

Allow yourself to mentally become close to this horse. In your mind imagine yourself next to the horse, facing the same direction. Be so close that, even though you are not touching, your auras blend. Slide sideways and gently become one with the horse. *PAUSE FOR 20 SECONDS* Look through your eyes. *PAUSE FOR 20 SECONDS* Feel your ears, and listen through them. Feel how they can move. *PAUSE FOR 20 SECONDS* Feel the weight of your body. *PAUSE FOR 20 SECONDS* Are you male or female? *PAUSE FOR 5 SECONDS*

Be outside in a field. Feel your hooves on the grass. *PAUSE FOR 10 SECONDS* Move around and experience how it feels. *PAUSE FOR 20 SECONDS*

Be aware of the smells around you. *PAUSE FOR 10 SECONDS* Listen to sounds, and notice how acute your hearing is.   *PAUSE FOR 10 SECONDS*   Put your head down and experience eating grass. Move leisurely as you graze.   *PAUSE FOR 30 SECONDS*   See a stream and drink.   *PAUSE FOR 10 SECONDS*

Find a patch of ground that is made of gritty soil, just right to scratch and clean you.   *PAUSE FOR 10 SECONDS*   Blow through your nostrils to see if dust will rise.   *PAUSE FOR 5 SECONDS.*   Nose around for the best spot. When you find it, bend your front legs and lower your body to the ground.   *PAUSE FOR 15 SECONDS*   Roll onto your side and grind your body delightfully into the gritty soil.   *PAUSE FOR 20 SECONDS*   Kick hard to roll over and do the other side.   *PAUSE FOR 20 SECONDS*

Be still now and feel the rays of sun warming you. Be centered and grounded so you can feel the motion of the earth as it rotates. Be one with the universe. Feel energy entering your body.   *PAUSE FOR 30 SECONDS*

Roll back onto your belly, put your front legs in front of you, and dig your front hooves into the ground and pull yourself to a standing position.   *PAUSE FOR 10 SECONDS*   Shake the loose dirt from your body.   *PAUSE FOR 10 SECONDS*   Take off, running, bucking, and snorting, as the energy flows through you.   *PAUSE FOR 15 SECONDS*   See a grassy place that appeals to you. Stop running. Lower your head, choose the best grass and start grazing. *PAUSE FOR 20 SECONDS*

See other horses walking toward you. Do you want to be with them? *PAUSE FOR 10 SECONDS* The other horses start to gallop. Join them. Run and kick. *PAUSE FOR 10 SECONDS* Stop and eat near the other horses by an outcropping of rocks. *PAUSE FOR 20 SECONDS*

See a mountain lion on the rocks. He is about to jump onto your back. *PAUSE FOR 2 SECONDS* Run! *PAUSE FOR 10 SECONDS* Go to a safe place and settle down. *PAUSE FOR 20 SECONDS* See humans. *PAUSE FOR 5 SECONDS* If you want to be with them, approach them. If not, just observe them. *PAUSE FOR 10 SECONDS*

Is there any message you would like to give to the humans? *PAUSE FOR 20 SECONDS* Did they understand? *PAUSE FOR 10 SECONDS*

Take a deep breath and move back to your own human body. *PAUSE FOR 20 SECONDS* Look at the horse and see how you feel now. *PAUSE FOR 10 SECONDS* Thank the horse for the help and guidance. *PAUSE FOR 10 SECONDS*

Return now to your physical surrounding, open your eyes and take one more deep breath.

MEDITATION ON BEING A RACCOON

I was helped with this meditation by a raccoon in the woods near my home. She wants us to live in harmony with nature. She was concerned with the quality of air and water, and wants us to stop changing the balance of the planet.

Sit in a comfortable position. Do not cross your legs, feet, or arms. Close your eyes and take three deep breaths. *PAUSE FOR 20 SECONDS* Allow yourself to breathe deeply and normally. Feel your brow relax. *PAUSE FOR 10 SECONDS* Relax your jaw. *PAUSE FOR 10 SECONDS* Feel your shoulders loosen and drop. *PAUSE FOR 10 SECONDS* Feel your stomach muscles relax. *PAUSE FOR 10 SECONDS* Allow the relaxation to flow down your body. As you breathe out ask that any negative energy be removed. Let any negative thoughts flow down through your body, out through your feet, and be sent into the universe to be reversed into positive energy. Know, as you breathe in, this is a gentle and loving way to get to know an animal.

Imagine you have a door at the base of your breast bone. *PAUSE FOR 5 SECONDS* Allow the door to open wide to allow the communication to flow from the raccoon to you.

Continue to breathe deeply, and now ask a raccoon to be your guide and teacher and to help you. Ask this raccoon

MEDITATION ON BEING A RACCOON

to appear to you. *PAUSE FOR 30 SECONDS* Observe the raccoon. See the blend of colors that form the stripes, and texture of the raccoon's coat. *PAUSE 10 SECONDS* Note the mask. *PAUSE FOR 10 SECONDS* See the nose and eyes. *PAUSE FOR 10 SECONDS*

Allow yourself to mentally become close to this raccoon. In your mind imagine yourself next to the raccoon, facing the same direction. Be so close that, even though you are not touching, your auras blend. Slide sideways and gently become one with the raccoon. Are you male or female? *PAUSE FOR 10 SECONDS* How old are you? *PAUSE FOR 10 SECONDS*

Look through your eyes. *PAUSE FOR 20 SECONDS* Feel your ears, and listen through them. *PAUSE FOR 10 SECONDS* Notice how acute your hearing is. Feel how the ears can move and rotate. *PAUSE FOR 20 SECONDS* Feel the weight of your body. *PAUSE FOR 20 SECONDS* Feel your paws on the surface on which you stand. Move around and experience how it feels. Climb up a fence post and walk along the rail. *PAUSE FOR 20 SECONDS* Feel your tail, and make it move.

Be aware of the aromas around you. *PAUSE FOR 10 SECONDS* See a stream with wild berries growing on the banks. *PAUSE FOR 10 SECONDS* Pick a berry and wash it in the clear water. *PAUSE FOR 30 SECONDS* Eat the cool clean berry. *PAUSE FOR 20 SECONDS* Lick your paws and your fur. *PAUSE FOR 20 SECONDS*

See a trash bag in a can. *PAUSE FOR 10 SECONDS* Climb up the can and start tearing the trash bag. *PAUSE FOR 15 SECONDS* See a dog bearing down on you. Run to a tree. *PAUSE FOR 5 SECONDS* Climb the tree and watch the dog go away. Make sure he is gone. *PAUSE FOR 10 SECONDS* Climb down and go to your nest in your tree. *PAUSE FOR 20 SECONDS*

While you are in your nest see some humans walking nearby. *PAUSE FOR 10 SECONDS* How do you feel about them. Is there anything you would like to tell them?

Take a deep breath and move back to your own human body. *PAUSE FOR 20 SECONDS* Look at the raccoon and see how you feel now. *PAUSE FOR 10 SECONDS* Thank the raccoon for the help and guidance. *PAUSE FOR 20 SECONDS*

Return now to your physical surrounding, open your eyes and take one more deep breath.

MEDITATION ON BEING A SNAKE

I had almost finished the book, but I had the feeling that I should include another meditation in it. I centered myself and asked who wanted to talk to me. I could feel the presence of a small snake. She wanted to tell me there should be a meditation about reptiles in the book. She said she was important to the ecology and should not be overlooked. I promised her a place with the other animals.

Sit in a comfortable position. Do not cross your legs, feet, or arms. Close your eyes and take three deep breaths. *PAUSE FOR 20 SECONDS* Allow yourself to breathe deeply and normally. Feel your brow relax. *PAUSE FOR 10 SECONDS* Relax your jaw. *PAUSE FOR 10 SECONDS* Feel your shoulders loosen and drop. *PAUSE FOR 10 SECONDS* Feel your stomach muscles relax. *PAUSE FOR 10 SECONDS* Allow the relaxation to flow down your body. As you breathe out ask that any negative energy be removed. Negative thoughts can flow down through your body, out through your feet, and be released into the universe to be reversed into positive energy. Know, as you breathe in, this is a gentle and loving way to get to know an animal.

Imagine you have a door at the base of your breastbone. *PAUSE FOR 5 SECONDS* Allow the door to open wide to allow the communication to flow from the snake to you.

Continue to breathe deeply, and now ask a snake to

be your guide and teacher and to help you. Ask this snake to appear to you. *PAUSE FOR 30 SECONDS* Observe the snake. See the snake's color or colors, and the design on the scales. *PAUSE FOR 10 SECONDS* See the eyes and darting tongue. *PAUSE FOR 10 SECONDS*

Allow yourself to mentally become close to this snake. In your mind imagine yourself next to the snake, facing the same direction. Be so close that, even though you are not touching, your auras blend. Slide sideways and gently become one with the snake. *PAUSE FOR 20 SECONDS*

Are you male or female? *PAUSE FOR 10 SECONDS* How old are you? *PAUSE FOR 10 SECONDS* Look through your eyes. *PAUSE FOR 10 SECONDS* Feel the length and thickness of your body. *PAUSE FOR 10 SECONDS* Are you male or female? *PAUSE FOR 5 SECONDS* Do you have sacs with poison in your mouth? *PAUSE FOR 5 SECONDS*

Glide to a sunny, warm rock, and feel the heat on your underside. *PAUSE FOR 10 SECONDS* Feel the contour of the rock as you coil your body to absorb the warmth of the sun. *PAUSE FOR 10 SECONDS* Flick your tongue in and out to sense the energy, motion, and smells around you. *PAUSE FOR 5 SECONDS* Use the muscles in your body to move forward to tall grass. *PAUSE FOR 10 SECONDS* Continue going forward, winding through the clumps of grass and weeds. *PAUSE FOR 10 SECONDS* Raise up and see over the grass. *PAUSE FOR 5 SECONDS* See a large predator coming toward you. *PAUSE FOR 2 SECONDS* Escape! Race into a hole in the ground. *PAUSE FOR 10 SECONDS*

Come out when the predator has gone, and make your way to a nearby stream. *PAUSE FOR 10 SECONDS*

Slide in the water and swim to the other side. *PAUSE FOR 10 SECONDS* Glide up the bank and see a mouse. *PAUSE FOR 5 SECONDS* Stay very still as the mouse comes near you. *PAUSE FOR 15 SECONDS* Feel the ground vibrate. The mouse scurries off, and humans are approaching. *PAUSE FOR 5 SECONDS* How do you feel about them? Is there any message you would like to give them? *PAUSE FOR 20 SECONDS*

Take a deep breath and move back to your own human body. *PAUSE FOR 10 SECONDS* Look at the snake and see how you feel now. *PAUSE FOR 10 SECONDS*

Thank the snake for the guidance. *PAUSE FOR 10 SECONDS*

Return now to your physical surrounding, open your eyes and take one more deep breath.

MEDITATIONS ON ANIMALS YOU KNOW

You can do this exercise either with or without a photograph. It would be best to do it first using a photograph, and then a second meditation without one. The process is the same whether the animal is living or deceased.

When you use a photograph do the following: Study the animal's physical appearance. Note the position of the body and expression on its face. Cup your hand and put it over the photos. (If you put your hand flat you will get prints on the picture.) You may or may not get a tingling feeling in your hand. It does not matter if you do not feel anything unusual.

Close your eyes and take the three deep breaths, as you have done for all the other meditations, to center yourself. Say the animal's name to yourself and ask for a communication. Turn on the tape recording you have made from the following pages in this chapter and proceed with the exercise.

If you are not using a photograph, close your eyes and start with the three deep breaths to center yourself. Say the animal's name to yourself and ask for a communication. Then turn on the tape recording you have made from the following pages in this chapter and proceed with the exercise.

I have mentioned remembering areas of pain or soreness as you do the exercises. This will aid you when it is time to get professional help to treat your animal. You will know the location and type of discomfort, such as: throbbing, sharp, intermittent, etc.

MEDITATION TO BE A CAT YOU KNOW

Sit in a comfortable position. Do not cross your legs, feet, or arms. Close your eyes and take three deep breaths to center and relax yourself. *PAUSE FOR 20 SECONDS* Allow yourself to breathe deeply and normally. Feel your brow relax. *PAUSE FOR 10 SECONDS* Relax your jaw. *PAUSE FOR 10 SECONDS* Feel your shoulders loosen and drop. *PAUSE FOR 10 SECONDS* Feel your stomach muscles relax. *PAUSE FOR 10 SECONDS* Allow the relaxation to flow down your body. As you breathe out ask that any negative energy be removed. Let the negative thoughts flow down through your body, out through your feet, and be released into the universe to be reversed into positive energy. Know, as you breathe in, this is a gentle and loving way to get to know this animal.

Imagine you have a door at the base of your breastbone. *PAUSE FOR 5 SECONDS* Allow the door to open wide to allow the communication to flow from the cat to you.

Continue to breathe deeply, and now ask a cat you know to talk to you. Ask this cat to appear to you. *PAUSE FOR 30 SECONDS* Observe the cat. You may get the information by seeing, feeling, or sensing. As you travel through the body, remember any areas that feel sore so you can consult the veterinarian later, if needed, when you are finished with the exercise.

Note the condition of the coat, whether shiny or dull. *PAUSE FOR 10 SECONDS*   Be aware of the nose and eyes.   *PAUSE FOR 10 SECONDS*

Allow yourself to mentally become close to this cat. In your mind imagine yourself next to the cat, facing the same direction. Be so close that, even though you are not touching, your auras blend. Slide sideways and gently become one with the cat.   *PAUSE FOR 20 SECONDS*   Look through your eyes.   *PAUSE FOR 10 SECONDS*   Know your ears and how they can move.   Listen through them.   *PAUSE FOR 10 SECONDS*   Be aware of the sharpness of your front teeth, and the length of the canines.   *PAUSE FOR 10 SECONDS*   Sniff through your nose, and know how sensitive the sense of smell is.

Move to the spine, and travel down the length of your neck, seeing, sensing, or feeling the vertebrae. Go to the base of your neck. Is there any pain or discomfort?   *PAUSE FOR 20 SECONDS*   Move down the left side of your shoulder and to your elbow.   *PAUSE FOR 10 SECONDS*   Continue down your left front leg, feeling, sensing, seeing.   *PAUSE FOR 10 SECONDS*   Move slowly down past your knee and on down your lower leg to your paw.   *PAUSE FOR 10 SECONDS*   Has there been any pain or discomfort? Be aware of your paw - the joints of the toes.   *PAUSE FOR 10 SECONDS*   Feel the pads.   *PAUSE FOR 5 SECONDS*   Now travel slowly up your leg, being aware of muscles and tendons.   *PAUSE FOR 15 SECONDS*   Continue up from your leg, and return to your spine. Travel slowly down your spine to the hips. Note any pain.   *PAUSE FOR 20 SECONDS*   Be aware of the place where your hips join the spine.   *PAUSE FOR 10 SECONDS*   Move out to the point of your left hip.   *PAUSE FOR 5 SECONDS*

Sense, feel, see. Move down your left hind leg to the first joint at the stifle.   *PAUSE FOR 10 SECONDS*   Continue down the hock, or knee at the back of your leg.   *PAUSE FOR 5 SECONDS*   Now move down your lower leg to the paw.   *PAUSE FOR 10 SECONDS*   Feel your toe joints, and then the pads.   *PAUSE FOR 5 SECONDS*   Travel slowly up your leg, being aware of muscles and tendons.   *PAUSE FOR 15 SECONDS*

Return to your spine, and move toward the tail.   *PAUSE FOR 5 SECONDS*   Does everything feel the way it should? Come back to your right hip and travel slowly down the bones of the leg to the paw.   *PAUSE FOR 35 SECONDS*   Return up your right hind leg, being aware of muscles and tendons.   *PAUSE FOR 15 SECONDS*

Return to your spine and move forward to your right front leg.   *PAUSE FOR 15 SECONDS*   Go down the front leg to the paw.   *PAUSE FOR 35 SECONDS*   Return up your right front leg slowly, being aware of muscles and tendons.   *PAUSE FOR 10 SECONDS*   Move to your right shoulder.   *PAUSE FOR 5 SECONDS*

Feel your rib cage.   *PAUSE FOR 10 SECONDS* Be aware of your heart as it pumps blood with a regular cadence.   *PAUSE FOR 20 SECONDS*   Feel your lungs as they fill with air and then expel it.   *PAUSE FOR 20 SECONDS*   Know the feeling of your stomach. Is it full or empty?   *PAUSE FOR 10 SECONDS*   Understand the placement of the organs within your body, and feel, see, or know how they work.   *PAUSE FOR 30 SECONDS*

Walk around and feel the bones, muscles and tendons as you move.   *PAUSE FOR 30 SECONDS*   Arch your back.   *PAUSE FOR 10 SECONDS*   Sit down, then stand again.   *PAUSE FOR 20 SECONDS*   Jump onto a wide window sill and lie down.   *PAUSE FOR 10 SECONDS*

Take a deep breath and move back to your own human body.   *PAUSE FOR 20 SECONDS*   Look at the cat and remind yourself of any places that were painful or uncomfortable. *PAUSE FOR 10 SECONDS* Thank the cat for the help and guidance. *PAUSE FOR 10 SECONDS*

Return now to your physical surrounding, open your eyes and take one more deep breath.

MEDITATION TO BE A DOG YOU KNOW

Sit in a comfortable position. Do not cross your legs, feet, or arms. Close your eyes and take three deep breaths to center and relax yourself. *PAUSE FOR 20 SECONDS* Allow yourself to breathe deeply and normally. Feel your brow relax. *PAUSE FOR 10 SECONDS* Relax your jaw. *PAUSE FOR 10 SECONDS* Feel your shoulders loosen and drop. *PAUSE FOR 10 SECONDS* Feel your stomach muscles relax. *PAUSE FOR 10 SECONDS* Allow the relaxation to flow down your body. As you breathe out ask that any negative energy be removed. Let the negative thoughts flow down through your body, out through your feet, and be released into the universe to be reversed into positive energy. Know, as you breathe in, this is a gentle and loving way to get to know this animal.

Imagine you have a door at the base of your breastbone. *PAUSE FOR 5 SECONDS* Allow the door to open wide to allow the communication to flow from the dog to you.

Continue to breathe deeply, and now ask a dog you know to come to you. Ask this dog to appear to you. *PAUSE FOR 30 SECONDS* Observe the dog. You may get the information by seeing, feeling, or sensing.

MEDITATION TO BE A DOG YOU KNOW

As you travel through the body, remember any areas that feel sore so you can consult the veterinarian later, if needed, when you are finished with the exercise.

Note the condition of the coat, whether shiny or dull. *PAUSE FOR 10 SECONDS* Be aware of the nose and eyes. *PAUSE FOR 10 SECONDS*

Allow yourself to mentally become close to this dog. In your mind imagine yourself next to the dog, facing the same direction. Be so close that, even though you are not touching, your auras blend. Slide sideways and gently become one with the dog. *PAUSE FOR 20 SECONDS* Look through your eyes. *PAUSE FOR 10 SECONDS* Know your ears and how they can move. Listen through them. *PAUSE FOR 10 SECONDS* Be aware of the sharpness of your front teeth, and the length of the canines. *PAUSE FOR 10 SECONDS* Sniff through your nose, and know how sensitive the sense of smell is.

Move to the spine, and travel down the length of your neck, seeing, sensing, or feeling the vertebrae. Go to the base of your neck. Is there any pain or discomfort? *PAUSE FOR 20 SECONDS* Move down the left side of your shoulder and to your elbow. *PAUSE FOR 10 SECONDS* Continue down your left front leg, feeling, sensing, seeing. *PAUSE FOR 10 SECONDS* Move slowly down past your knee and on down your lower leg to your paw. *PAUSE FOR 10 SECONDS* Has there been any pain or discomfort? Be aware of your paw - the joints of the toes. *PAUSE FOR 10 SECONDS* Feel the pads. *PAUSE FOR 5 SECONDS* Now travel slowly up your leg, being aware of muscles and tendons. *PAUSE FOR 15 SECONDS* Continue up from your leg, and return to your spine. Travel slowly down your spine to the hips. Note any pain. *PAUSE FOR 20 SECONDS* Be aware of the place where your hips join the spine. *PAUSE FOR 10 SECONDS* Move out to the point of your left hip. *PAUSE FOR 5 SECONDS*

Sense, feel, see. Move down your left hind leg to the first joint at the stifle. *PAUSE FOR 10 SECONDS* Continue down the hock, or knee at the back of your leg. *PAUSE FOR 5 SECONDS* Now move down your lower leg to the paw. *PAUSE FOR 10 SECONDS* Feel your toe joints, and then the pads. *PAUSE FOR 5 SECONDS* Travel slowly up your leg, being aware of muscles and tendons. *PAUSE FOR 15 SECONDS*

Return to your spine, and move toward the tail. *PAUSE FOR 5 SECONDS* Does everything feel the way it should? Come back to your right hip and travel slowly down the bones of the leg to the paw. *PAUSE FOR 35*

MEDITATION TO BE A DOG YOU KNOW

SECONDS   Return up your right hind leg, being aware of muscles and tendons. *PAUSE FOR 15 SECONDS*   Return to your spine and move forward to your right front leg. *PAUSE FOR 15 SECONDS*   Go down the front leg to the paw. *PAUSE FOR 35 SECONDS*   Return up your right front leg slowly, being aware of muscles and tendons. *PAUSE FOR 10 SECONDS*   Move to your right shoulder. *PAUSE FOR 5 SECONDS*

Feel your rib cage. *PAUSE FOR 10 SECONDS* Be aware of your heart as it pumps blood with a regular cadence. *PAUSE FOR 20 SECONDS*   Feel your lungs as they fill with air and then expel it. *PAUSE FOR 20 SECONDS*   Know the feeling of your stomach. Is it full or empty? *PAUSE FOR 10 SECONDS*   Understand the placement of the organs within your body, and feel, see, or know how they work. *PAUSE FOR 30 SECONDS*

Walk around and feel the bones, muscles and tendons as you move. *PAUSE FOR 30 SECONDS*   Wag your tail. *PAUSE FOR 10 SECONDS*   Sit down, then stand again. *PAUSE FOR 20 SECONDS*   Shake your body as if it was wet. *PAUSE FOR 10 SECONDS*

Take a deep breath and move back to your own human body. *PAUSE FOR 20 SECONDS*   Look at the dog and remind yourself of any places that were painful or uncomfortable. *PAUSE FOR 10 SECONDS* Thank the dog for the help and guidance. *PAUSE FOR 10 SECONDS*

Return now to your physical surrounding, open your eyes and take one more deep breath.

MEDITATION TO BE A HORSE YOU KNOW

Sit in a comfortable position. Do not cross your legs, feet, or arms. Close your eyes and take three deep breaths to center and relax yourself. *PAUSE FOR 20 SECONDS* Allow yourself to breathe deeply and normally. Feel your brow relax. *PAUSE FOR 10 SECONDS* Relax your jaw. *PAUSE FOR 10 SECONDS* Feel your shoulders loosen and drop. *PAUSE FOR 10 SECONDS* Feel your stomach muscles relax. *PAUSE FOR 10 SECONDS* Allow the relaxation to flow down your body. As you breathe out ask that any negative energy be removed. Let the negative thoughts flow down through your body, out through your feet, and be released into the universe to be reversed into positive energy. Know, as you breathe in, this is a gentle and loving way to get to know this animal.

Imagine you have a door at the base of your breastbone. *PAUSE FOR 5 SECONDS* Allow the door to open wide to allow the communication to flow from the horse to you.

Continue to breathe deeply, and now ask a horse you know to come talk to you. Ask this horse to appear to you. *PAUSE FOR 30 SECONDS* Observe the horse. You may get the information by seeing, feeling, or sensing. As you travel through the body, remember any areas that feel sore so you can consult the veterinarian later, if needed, when you are finished with the exercise.

Note the condition of the coat, whether shiny or dull. *PAUSE FOR 10 SECONDS*   Be aware of the nose and eyes.   *PAUSE FOR 10 SECONDS*

Allow yourself to mentally become close to this horse. In your mind imagine yourself next to the horse, facing the same direction. Be so close that, even though you are not touching, your auras blend. Slide sideways and gently become one with the horse. *PAUSE FOR 20 SECONDS*   Look through your eyes. *PAUSE FOR 10 SECONDS*   Know your ears and how they can move. Listen through them. *PAUSE FOR 10 SECONDS*   Be aware of the density of your teeth. *PAUSE FOR 10 SECONDS*   Sniff through your nose, and know how sensitive the sense of smell is.

Move to the spine, and travel down the length of your neck, seeing, sensing, or feeling the vertebrae. Go to the base of your neck. Is there any pain or discomfort? *PAUSE FOR 20 SECONDS*   Move down the left side of your shoulder and to your elbow. *PAUSE FOR 10 SECONDS*   Continue down your left front leg, feeling, sensing, seeing. *PAUSE FOR 10 SECONDS*   Move slowly down past your knee and on down your lower leg to your hoof. *PAUSE FOR 10 SECONDS*   Are you wearing shoes? Has there been any pain or discomfort? *PAUSE FOR 5 SECONDS* Now travel slowly up your leg, being aware of muscles and tendons. *PAUSE FOR 15 SECONDS* Continue up from your leg, and return to your spine. Travel slowly down your spine to the hips. Note any pain. *PAUSE FOR 20 SECONDS* Be aware of the place where your hips join the spine. *PAUSE FOR 10 SECONDS* Move out to the point of your left hip. *PAUSE FOR 5 SECONDS* Sense, feel, see. Move down your left hind leg to the first joint at the stifle. *PAUSE FOR 10 SECONDS* Continue down the hock, or knee at the back of your leg. *PAUSE FOR 5 SECONDS* Now move down your lower leg to the hoof. *PAUSE FOR 10 SECONDS* Travel slowly up your leg, being aware of muscles and tendons. *PAUSE FOR 15 SECONDS*

Return to your spine, and move toward the tail. *PAUSE FOR 5 SECONDS* Does everything feel the way it should? Come back to your right hip and travel slowly down the bones of the leg to the hoof. *PAUSE FOR 35 SECONDS* Return up your right hind leg, being aware of muscles and tendons. *PAUSE FOR 15 SECONDS*

Return to your spine and move forward to your right front leg. *PAUSE FOR 15 SECONDS* Go down the front leg to the hoof. *PAUSE FOR 35 SECONDS* Return up your right front leg slowly, being

MEDITATION TO BE A HORSE YOU KNOW

aware of muscles and tendons. *PAUSE FOR 10 SECONDS* Move to your right shoulder. *PAUSE FOR 5 SECONDS*

Feel your rib cage. *PAUSE FOR 10 SECONDS* Be aware of your heart as it pumps blood with a regular cadence. *PAUSE FOR 20 SECONDS* Feel your lungs as they fill with air and then expel it. *PAUSE FOR 20 SECONDS* Know the feeling of your stomach. Is it full or empty? *PAUSE FOR 10 SECONDS* Understand the placement of the organs within your body, and feel, see, or know how they work. *PAUSE FOR 30 SECONDS*

Walk around and feel the bones, muscles and tendons as you move. *PAUSE FOR 30 SECONDS* Move your head and neck. *PAUSE FOR 10 SECONDS* Paw the ground with your right front hoof. *PAUSE FOR 20 SECONDS* Stretch your body to relax. *PAUSE FOR 10 SECONDS*

Take a deep breath and move back to your own human body. *PAUSE FOR 20 SECONDS* Look at the horse and remind yourself of any places that were painful or uncomfortable. *PAUSE FOR 10 SECONDS* Thank the horse for the help and guidance. *PAUSE FOR 10 SECONDS*

Return now to your physical surrounding, open your eyes and take one more deep breath.

HEARING THE ANIMALS

Now that the ground work is done and you have practiced some of the meditations and become like the various animals, it is time to have a conversation with an animal. You may receive answers in the form of pictures in your mind, discomfort or pain, sudden knowledge (you just <u>know</u>), or words. Some people receive emotions, smells, or even colors.

I experience many different ways of receiving information during a communication. I always hear my own voice in my head. It is similar to when I wonder about something and I can hear the words in my mind, such as: "Did I lock the door?" When I hear the answers from the animals, I usually feel the emotion: lighthearted, depressed, angry, etc. Sometimes I see pictures. They may be still or moving, or of an event happening. When communicating with a missing animal I look through its eyes to see what surrounds it. I also ask questions that are answered in words.

Some animals like to carry on long conversations, and others are rather abrupt and give information with as few words as possible.

When you talk to the animals they receive much of the conversation in pictures. There is no picture for any negative word, such as: don't, not, can't. If you are told, "Don't think of five bananas that are slightly green," it is almost impossible to keep that picture of those green bananas out of your mind. Therefore, you must say positive words to the animals. "Don't run in the street," should be presented as, "Stay in the yard." The first way shows the animal a picture of him running in the street, the second way shows him a picture of staying in the yard.

No matter how you receive information, it is correct. Accept it.

If you do not understand what the animal is telling you, ask for clarification.

The first few times you communicate with animals it is helpful to work with a partner and talk to that person's animal. It is always important to get verification.

Working With a Partner

Ask the other person to write the questions and take notes. You can then concentrate on the communication.

Take deep breaths to center yourself. Be calm in mind and body, and open the doors at your breastbone. Look at a photo, if one is available, or ask your partner questions about the animal (name, age, sex, color). It is better not to ask questions about health or emotions so you receive those answers without feeling you have been "prompted."

You can ask questions mentally or out loud. Either way is correct. First, ask the animal for permission to talk to him. If the answer is "no," say thank you, and do not ask any more questions. You may try again later when the animal can trust you more, or when he has become used to the idea of a human talking to him. Many animals who have been abused do not believe humans can be honest and caring.

When I get permission to talk to the animal, I usually ask, "How do you feel?" or "Is there anything you would like to tell me?" Relate the questions and answers to your partner so she can take notes.

Always remember to thank the animal before you end the conversation.

Working Alone

The process of communication is the same as when you work with another person. You can write your questions and make notes when you receive answers, or you use a tape recorder to keep track of your communications.

Wrap Yourself In White Light

Each morning when I wake I thank my higher powers for that day. I also surround myself with a white light and ask that only true and accurate information will be received during communications. I include the request that I may deliver that information in a caring, compassionate manner. I repeat this every night before I sleep. You may want to center yourself before each communication, sometimes I'm too busy to do this between calls, so the morning and evening works better for me. If you become frazzled it is a good idea to center yourself before you continue.

It is also <u>very important</u> to know you may experience the pain of the animal with whom you are communicating. If this pain continues after the conversation has ended, ask your higher power to remove it. I usually ask: "That pain that is not mine, please be removed from my body." I have found this to be quite effective, but you may alter it to whatever suits you.

Missing Animals

A challenging animal communication is with animals who are lost or stolen. The telepathic connection is difficult because both the animal and the person are very emotional. Since there is no time or distance in telepathy, when the animal says where it is "now," may not be "now" to you. Sometimes it is the previous hour or the previous day. It is difficult for me to tell if the animal is dead or alive, but some people can.

You can still ask questions of the animal. I am always expanding my list of questions to ask an animal. The following are some suggestions: Did you cross a road/stream/field/ etc.? Are there trees? Are you inside or outside of the house? If you are inside, what can you see from the windows? Can you see the road? Who lives in the house? What names do the people call each other? Are there other animals in the house? If you're outside, are you near any buildings? Describe them. Can they be seen from the road? Are you wearing a collar and tag? If so, please let someone read it. Were you out hunting something when you got lost or were you chased? Did a person take you? Describe the person. Did you get in a vehicle? Describe the vehicle.

I also encourage people to put up posters. Sometimes a helpful person recognizes the lost animal. It is a good idea to enlist the help of school children. They are usually aware of new animals in the neighborhood, and can also ask their school friends if a stray is in the area.

Things Can Change

An animal may tell you when he thinks he is going to die. Before you say anything, remind yourself that Things Can Change, and choose your words carefully. However, it is important that you convey the seriousness of the situation. Their messages may actually be, "I'm so depressed I want to die," or "Unless my problem is fixed it will kill me." I was told my horse Colonel was going to die "in June." Before June arrived we discovered and fixed a problem with his teeth. Perhaps he would have died in June if we had not corrected the problem. As I write this four years later Colonel is grazing outside my office window.

Sometimes an animal plans to die at a particular time but changes his plans, like our pony, Sally. When she was quite old and arthritic she told a communicator she would die in March. When she lived past March I had the communicator thank Sally for still being with us, and ask her what happened. Sally explained she intended to die in March, but learned our dog, Puppy, would die soon. She said she did not want to sadden our family by having both of them leave so close together, so she would wait until the following March. Puppy died that May, and Sally did indeed die the following March.

Although the communicator accurately told us Sally's intentions, Sally's plans had changed. I would have preferred not to have spent a year anticipating her death. You must use your own judgment when confronted by a similar situation. My personal preference is to avoid these discussions. I remind people that my skills are to discuss past and present, not future.

Saying Farewell

One of the greatest services you can do for a pet and his person is to help them communicate with each other when the animal is ready to depart from this life. This is different from predicting the time of death in advance.

The final decisions are up to the animal and his person. Some animals request euthanasia, and may even have a preference about where it takes place, such as at home. Some animals want the person to be with them, and others prefer to spare their person the pain of dealing with the death. Many animals choose to wait until the person is away from them to make the transition. Some owners ask how the animal feels about cremation or burial. For the most part, I have found some animals have a preference, but most do not, they are just ready to be rid of the body that is no longer doing its job.

Another important service is to help a person say farewell after an animal has already died. There are times when we are not able to be with our pets when they die — we are away on a trip, or the pet is at the veterinarian's. We suffer guilt and wonder if the animal needed us at the end. There is closure for the grieving person if he can hear what his animal companion has to say, and guilt can be relieved if the animal passed gently. There are several stories in my book *Animal Wisdom* that tell of the feelings of animals who are about to pass or who have passed.

Reincarnation

Religious beliefs vary widely about reincarnation, and sometimes people just reject the idea. If the person asks if her friend will be "back" I ask the pet and answer freely.

I also have clients who ask about former lives with their animals. This can be a lot of fun to explore. My book *Animal Wisdom* has a chapter with stories of people's experiences with reincarnation of their animal friends.

Saying Thank You

Be sure you always acknowledge the help the animal has given you. I always start my communications by asking if I may please talk to the animal, and finish by thanking him. If the animal does not care to communicate, I thank him anyway. The courtesies we show each other should be shown to the animals, too.

Enjoy The Communications!

FLOWER ESSENCES
BY CELESTE CARUSO

Communication with the animal kingdom has great value for many obvious reasons. For instance, it's a great way to find out what makes our pets tick emotionally. Are they content and happy? Are they frustrated or depressed? You will be able to learn from your pets the origin of their distress. Once you learn the skills taught to you so wonderfully in this book, you can help them with their behavioral problems. The purpose of this chapter is to help you. This help comes in the form of a floral bouquet.

As you may know, Mother Nature has provided us with all that we need to heal ourselves and all creatures on the planet. One of her most treasured gifts is flowers. The beauty of flowers is not only in their scent, color, and shape, but also in their "vibes." Like listening to a beautiful piece of music, they affect us on deeper levels to help us balance and heal. The essence of the flowers vibrate their goodness right to your very soul.

In the 1930's a physician named Dr. Edward Bach of London, England, developed the first line of flower essences. His work set the ground work for this unusual type of healing. As he practiced medicine he began to understand the importance of the state of mind in the patient's healing process. He observed that certain states of mind interfered with the true course or prime directive of one's life. These states, such as fear, uncertainty, and loneliness caused a great disruption in his patients general health and well-being. And, just as there were negative states, there were positive ones, such as Love, Joy, Faith and Peace, which brought his patients back to health. After experimenting with different flower essences he found that certain flower essences helped to achieve positive states of mind.

The flower essence formulations are simply water infused with the electromagnetic signature of the flower. This process is done in a natural setting where the blossom is picked at the most auspicious time and placed in a vat of spring water out in the sunshine. The vibration of the flower is transferred into the water, which will then make up the mother tincture once the blossoms are removed. Unlike essential oils used in Aromatherapy, no fragrance is released through the process. Instead, you get an odorless and colorless infusion, with no organic content except water and a small percentage of a preservative, like alcohol or glycerin. A remedy can be comprised of a single flower essence or a combination of various single flower essences blended together. Traditionally, no more than 5 single essences should be combined at one time. However, animals can handle more than five essences at a time as they are much more receptive. Unlike humans, they have no conscious mind to interfere with judgment about the effectiveness of the remedies, and they have no attachments to their illnesses.

These remedies are currently and successfully being used for behavior modification in animals, particularly dogs, cats, and horses. They are administered to correct unacceptable behavior such as aggression, willfulness, over-protectiveness of territory, obsessive self-mutilation, nervousness, intolerance of others and just plain annoying behavior. They're also used in animal shelters to bring stabilization to abused and abandoned animals to help them release fear and trauma. The soothing message of the flowers allows the rescued animal to experience a sense of safety and love from the rescuers. This has enabled them to achieve a normal state of emotional health.

FLOWER ESSENCES

As you know, your pet doesn't have to be from a shelter to have problems. There are many pet owners who find themselves at a loss when it comes to understanding their pet's behavioral "dysfunction." It does help to know the inside story, which you'll find out when you get in touch with them intuitively. I was a professional psychic for people for many years, so tuning in to the animals was easy. I also had years of experience consulting people on the use of flower remedies. In 1995, a trainer for thoroughbred racehorses asked me to check out a beautiful three year old colt he was training. The colt was fine when he was out of the stall, but as soon as he was returned to his stall after his morning routine, he freaked out. As I approached him in his stall I got the feeling of extreme terror. I told him I was there to help and asked him to show me how this condition came about. The horse then proceeded to show me a picture of himself, a memory, before he came to the racetrack. I picked up this picture in my mind's eye. (It's like watching a movie.) He was in his stall at night and something fell on his head. No one was there to see it, and it really didn't harm him; it just scared the living daylights out of him. I tried to comfort him and told him not to be afraid anymore. He was safe. I recommended to the trainer that he give the colt Dr. Bach's **Rescue Remedy** (the most well known flower essence remedy) or **FES' Five Flower Remedy**. Both remedies contain Impatiens, Star of Bethlehem, Cherry Plum, Rock Rose and Clematis. This five-flower remedy is widely used in emergency situations to address issues of shock, terror and trauma. Many rescue facilities for wildlife and domestic animals use it when they first receive the injured or abused animal. As you can see from the descriptive chart at the end of this chapter, this was the perfect remedy to give to this colt to bring him out of his state of terror. The remedy worked so well I was asked about another horse who had problems focusing when training on the track. He would get distracted when the other horses galloped by, so I made a special formula containing Clematis and Cerato. Within a couple of days he was no longer distracted and was able to train more easily.

Another trainer I knew had problems with a two year old filly who was in training and wouldn't eat all her food. She checked out fine when they examined her teeth and they also ruled out stomach ulcers. When I visited her I felt an overwhelming sadness in my heart. I asked if a stablemate, or anyone else she was attached to, had left recently. The trainer at first said no, but then recalled that when they left Saratoga to return to Belmont Racetrack, her groom had gone back to Mexico to visit his family. This was her first and only groom since she arrived from the farm. I explained to the trainer (I think it helped that the trainer was a woman) that she was heartbroken because she was "in love" with her groom and he was gone. I recommended a remedy of Bleeding Heart and Honeysuckle, and comforted her with soothing touches and sympathetic words. She was fine within 24 hours. Her depression was gone and she started eating normally again.

After spending several months at the racetrack speaking with other trainers I realized that there was a need for specific formulations to address the needs of competitive horses. At the time I was selling all natural equine supplements for a company called **Equilite, Inc**. The president and founder, Stacey Small, encouraged me to make these special blends under the **Equilite** label. Being a horsewoman and a former competitor herself, she also felt a need for these remedies in the show ring and the three day event industry. So, with the help and support of Team **Equilite**, we came out with formulations in 1997 called **Equi-Essences** ™. During the developmental stages, our panel of advisors determined there are twelve categories or challenges that a horse would encounter during its competitive life. From these categories, we determined the names of the formulation. They come in kits appropriately named. **"The Wonder Years"** kit includes: Mama's blend, Weanling, and Yearling to Two Year Olds in Training for the breeding farms. The **"Horses In Training"** kit includes: Lighten Up/Tone Down, Clear Thinking, Ego Builder, and Mellow Out. The **"Winning Ways"** kit includes: Get Psyched, Re-Charge, and Settle In/Shipper. We became the first to market a line of flower essences exclusively for horses.

Since it's public debut, **Equi-Essences**™ has received numerous testimonials and is gaining in popularity with veterinarians, trainers, owners and riders. They are experiencing great results and find them to be very effective for behavior modification in their horses. As the results happen in such a gentle way, it's hard to believe that only a couple of drops of the remedy used over a few weeks time can have such a profound and long lasting effect on these animals.

Among the testimonials we received, one was from a horse breeder/veterinarian who told us she used the formula developed for the weanling when the colt leaves its mother. She said the weaning process went so smoothly that there wasn't the usual emotional anguish that the mother and her young one experience.

Because **Equi-Essences**™ is doing so well we decided to formulate a line of remedies especially for cats, dogs, and other domestic pets named **Pet Essences**™. In one of the case histories where **Pet Essences**™ remedies are being field tested, there was a Dalmation that was rescued by a shelter in Maryland. He would jump the fence to attack the shelter attendants when they came near his cage. He was obviously very abused before they found him and would not allow human contact. He was unapproachable. After only three days on the remedies he not only allowed them in his cage, but let them approach him. Who knows what suffering this poor animal endured from his owner. But now, miraculously, there was this turn around in such a short period of time. (I truly believe there are little angels in these bottles.)

Another case history that had a very happy ending was a rescued dog that was buried alive in mud at a golf course in Pennsylvania. The woman who rescued him lived next to the golf course and had been rescuing dogs from there for years. It seems that it's a popular local dumping ground for unwanted pets. After many baths and a visit to the veterinarian, the dog looked as if he would survive. But his will to live wasn't there, and he had a vacant look in his eyes to indicate his sorry state. After a week on the flower essence formulation blended for abused and abandoned animals, he literally came back to life. In all her years of rescuing animals (thirty, I believe) she has never seen such a quick recovery from this type of emotional devastation. It usually took months, if ever, to recover. He became a loving and playful pet, and was named Danny by his heroine. He now lives with her and her household of animals (and this is after vowing that she would never take in another stray). The flower essences gave this dog another chance at life, and with it, the gift of love and healing.

As I mentioned at the beginning of this chapter, the beauty of flowers goes beyond their physical appearance and their fragrance. They are here on the planet as helpers from heaven to bless us and touch our hearts and spirits no matter what form we come in - the two leggeds, the four leggeds, the winged ones. As the Native Americans would say while offering their blessings and prayers, **"To All My Relations."**

A list of flower essences follows. Use what you have learned in this book to ask your animals to describe their problems. You may want to verify the information you receive by dowsing. Chapter 5 in Anita's book *Animal Wisdom* explains how to dowse. Read this list over, then decide, with your pet, which essences would be best suited. To create your own formulation you need to purchase small (1 - 2 oz.) dropper bottles, and fill them 7/8 full with spring water, and the rest of the way with a preservative such as apple cider vinegar or glycerin. (You can use brandy or grain alcohol, but in very small amounts.)

Place 3 drops of each flower essence from the mother tinctures into your dropper bottle. Because this is considered a vibrational healing modality, like homeopathy, this dilution will not lessen the potency of the essences. It would be more like an extension than a dilution. Shake the new bottle well and bless, then follow the administering directions:

Water - Place 2-5 drops of flower essence stock in the animal's water vessel, depending on size of the animal (cat or dog dish 2 drops, horses water bucket 4-5 drops). The water method works well with animals that have their own water supply and drink freely and regularly. Each sip of the water is considered a dose. It is not necessary that they finish the entire contents of the water by the end of the day. The stock bottles should be **shaken before each application** to sustain potency and fresh water is to be used in the vessel with each new placement of essences. This method is recommended in non-emergency situations. Use daily over a period of at least four weeks for best results.

Oral Administration - Place 1-4 of flower essence stock drops under the tongue*, inside the cheek, or rub on gums of the animal to ensure that it receives the flower essences. (For small dogs and cats use 1-2 drops, medium to large dogs use 2-3 drops, for horses use 3-4 drops). A dose syringe filled with water can also be used to administer the essences. It is important to administer the remedies in this rhythmic fashion because they work more effectively this way. Regular, rhythmic use of the flower remedies builds the strength of their catalytic action. Therefore, potency is increased, not by taking more drops at one time, but by using them on a frequent, consistent basis. The oral methods are most beneficial during emergency situations when the animal is under stress and shows signs of behavioral changes that are severe and problematic. The rhythm of administering in these instances should be as frequent as every hour until normal behavior returns.

Follow up with the water method if necessary to help alleviate the cause of the undesirable behavior.

Spray - Place 4-5 drops of flower essences in a sprayer bottle filled with spring water. The animal can be misted both on its body and in the air surrounding it. This method works well with frightened animals and those animals like cats that are sensitive to changes in their drinking water. **Shake before each use** to sustain potency and remember to use on a rhythmic basis.

FLOWER ESSENCES

Food - Four to five drops of the flower essence remedy can be placed on or in the animal's food. This method may work best for animals such as puppies that eat frequently during the day or animals that eat moist food.

Alternative - Place a couple of drops on the finger tip and rub into the animal's ear, nose or muzzle. Frequency would depend on the situation as explained above.

*Important Suggestions:

Do not allow dropper to touch mouth of animal because of the chance of contamination. If it does occur, wipe off dropper with an alcohol swab before placing it back into the dosage bottle. If possible, when administering the essences, allow for a quiet moment of receptivity.

AGRIMONY - Feeling tormented, especially from infestation, real or imagined. Putting on a brave face while suffering.

ARNICA - For recovery from shock or trauma, especially when there is a disassociation from the body due to physical trauma or injury.

ASPEN - For animals that spook easily - unknown fears.

BEECH - Helps to generate tolerance of people, other animals, places and things.

BLACKBERRY - When there's frustration over the inability to act out will or intention.

FLOWER ESSENCES

BLACK-EYED SUSAN - Unconsciously repeating abusive patterns toward oneself e.g. chewing or scratching a body part until it's raw, or plucking out feathers.

BORAGE - Lifts spirits, instills hope, and gives courage good to relieve depressed states.

BLEEDING HEART Helps to release emotional attachments when a loved one leaves (temporarily or permanently).

CENTAURY - For the animal that allows others to push them around and be last in the pecking order.

CERATO - For clarity of thought, for the "air head."

CHAMOMILE - To help soothe the savage beast. Can help with incessant barkers, especially when there are stomach problems.

CHERRY PLUM -For out of control behavior, at their wits end.

CHESTNUT BUD - When a mistake is made over and over again - helps to break bad habits.

CHICORY - Overly possessive of family members as a result will demand constant attention and/or exhibit behavior to manipulate and control.

CLEMATIS - Increases consciousness as well as the ability to focus.

FLOWER ESSENCES

COSMOS - For interspecies communications between all members of the family, animal and human alike. (Would help in your pursuit to be an animal communicator.)

CRAB APPLE - Feeling unclean even after an infestation of fleas or odors e.g. skunk spray. Add a few drops to a water sprayer to mist your pet and its environment.

DILL - For sensory congestion in a new or unfamiliar situation e.g. traveling.

ELM - Overwhelmed by any unpleasant experience i.e. dog grooming, bathing.

GENTIAN - For setbacks of any kind, mentally or physically.

GORSE - When there's a feeling of hopelessness and despondency.

HEATHER - Demands constant attention for fear of being left alone. Very self absorbed.

HOLLY - For feelings of jealousy. Also, for animals who have a tendency to bite or anger easily.

HONEYSUCKLE - Helps to let go of the past. For homesickness or bereavement.

IMPATIENS - For the overly anxious and nervous animal, ones that are easily annoyed and agitated.

FLOWER ESSENCES

LARCH - Helps build confidence and a sense of self-worth.

MARIPOSA LILY - To help reconnect to Mother's love when feeling unloved and unwanted.

MIMULUS - For known fears. For shy animals who hide from people.

MUSTARD - For depressed states that come and go suddenly.

OLIVE - To help restore after long physical ordeal.

PINE - For those that over please to gain love and acceptance.

PINK YARROW - Protects against negative feelings from others.

RED CHESTNUT - For the overly vigilant and worrisome animal.

ROCK ROSE - For the stubborn animal that refuses to "go with the flow," uncompromising and inflexible.

SELF HEAL - Catalyzes the inner healing powers.

SNAPDRAGON - Misplaced forces of will and aggression that comes through as biting and snapping.

FLOWER ESSENCES

STAR OF BETHLEHEM - For any kind of trauma, emotionally or physically - past or present.

SWEET CHESTNUT - For when they are at wit's end, helps prevent "burn out."

VERVAIN - For the very intense, hyperactive animal that needs a place to focus its energy. Also takes everything too seriously - needs to lighten up.

WALNUT - Helps adjust to new surroundings and circumstances. Helps them feel protected, safe and secure.

WATER VIOLET - When an animal prefers to be left alone and separates off by itself, very aloof.

WILD OAT - For when your animal is depressed and bored because of illness.

WILD ROSE -Helps to left spirits and bring out of withdrawal from grief or depression.

WILLOW - For resentment of any kind.

Bibliography

Anita Curtis has an extensive private animal communication practice. Consultations are available by appointment, and can be scheduled by calling (610) 327-3820. She also offers lectures, Level 1 and Level 2 workshops, and a Counseling Workshop. Anita has a newsletter which she sends free by request to her clients. To order additional copies of *How To Hear The Animals*, send $18.00 (U.S.) plus $2.00 s&h (PA residents only $21.08, includes sales tax) check or money order, to Anita Curtis, P.O. Box 182, Gilbertsville, PA 19525-0182. Credit card orders call (610) 327-3820. Quantity discounts available.

Animal Wisdom: Communications With Animals can be ordered as above, for $11.95 each (U.S.) plus $2.00 s&h (PA residents only $14.67, includes sales tax).

Further Suggested Reading:

Animal Talk: Interspecies Telepathic Communications, Penelope Smith, Pegasus Publications.

Communicating With Animals, The Spiritual Connection Between People and Animals, Arthur Myers, Contemporary Books.

Equilite, Inc., (Equi-Essences™ and Pet Essences™), Stacey Small and Celeste Caruso, 20 Prospect Ave., Ardsley, NY 10502. Ask for free Botanical Animal Catalog. 1-800-942-LITE - Fax: (914) 693-4956. Visit website at www.equilite.com.

Equine Acupressure - First-Aid With Your Fingertips, Ron and Linda Briel of The Balancing Touch (610) 794-9184.

Flower Essence Repertory, Patricia Kaminski and Richard Katz, Flower Essence Society.

Holistic Horse Newsletter, Quarterly publication for adjunctive therapies for horses. Contains articles on herbs, flower essences, equine massage, and other natural modalities. Call for free sample issue (914) 693-2553, or visit website at www.holistichorse.com.

The Tellington TTouch, Linda Tellington-Jones with Sybil Taylor, Viking.

Thinking In Pictures, and Other Reports From My Life With Autism, Temple Grandin, Doubleday.